Zapatista Stories
for Dreaming
An-Other World

Subcomandante Marcos

*translated with commentaries
by Colectivo Relámpago
(Lightning Collective)*

K

KAIROS

PM

Zapatista Stories for Dreaming An-Other World
Colectivo Relámpago © 2022
This edition © PM Press

ISBN: 978-1-62963-970-3 (paperback)
ISBN: 978-1-62963-985-7 (ebook)
Library of Congress Control Number: 2022931957

Cover design by John Yates/www.stealworks.com
Interior design by briandesign

10 9 8 7 6 5 4 3 2

PM Press
PO Box 23912
Oakland, CA 94623
www.pmpress.org

Printed in the USA

Translators' Note

Our name, "Colectivo Relámpago," or Lightning Collective, was chosen when we imagined producing a quick set of English translations to support a solidarity project initiated by the Zapatista secondary school in Oventic. But our name turned out to be ironic, since, rather than lightning, our speed has been that of the snail, or *caracol*, a recurrent Zapatista trope: *We advance, yes, but slowly*. We sought to translate in a way that preserved the liveliness of these Zapatista stories and ended up finding them infinitely fascinating and revelatory, the more we researched their context and associations for our translations and commentaries. Because our experience was so unusual and so unexpected, perhaps we also haven't wanted our collective to end—and so became very good at discovering "futures yet to be born, paths not yet walked, dawns yet to break."

All proceeds from the sale of this book will go directly to Zapatista communities.

Translated with commentaries by Colectivo Relámpago
Antonia Carcelén-Estrada, Margaret Cerullo, Marina Kaplan, and Zack Zucker
Amherst, MA, 2022

Contents

The Stories

The Commentaries

Foreword

"After the flame comes the smoke; after the smoke follows the word."

> —Subcomandante Marcos, "The Story of Noise and Silence"

Characters smoke a lot in Zapatista stories. Old Antonio, the *guerrilleros'* guide to Indigenous history, culture, and perspective, rolls cornhusk cigarettes, pauses in his narration of many of the tales here, looks into the fire, inhales and watches as smoke curls from his mouth into the air. Don Durito—a beetle-turned-political analyst and dreamer, foil for Subcomandante Marcos's ego, voice of conscience, and vehicle for allusions to other literary and popular traditions—smokes a pipe, steals tobacco, and leaves a trail. Marcos smokes a pipe and has his tobacco stolen, thus encountering the wise and comical beetle Durito.

The first time that smoking appears in this collection, it might seem to be simply a mechanism to move the story from point a to point b; another time, it seems a common thing, just something people do, perhaps strange, even shocking, where smoking is taboo but an ordinary activity nonetheless. It might seem to be the storyteller's way of giving his tale some air with an extra rhythmic beat, another literary device. One might read right past it—especially when confronted with a talking beetle who wears spectacles, reads the newspapers at a tiny desk, and comments on the nature of neoliberalism. Soon enough, though, through repetition, what is, in fact, a common thing *and* a literary device is clearly something more as well.

Emblems in emblematic stories invite questions. In the tradition of fable and myth, the breath of life, manifested in the spiral of smoke, predicates thought, which bursts into the world, carried on the air, in the word. The word made flesh, or corn in Maya cosmology; human beings, that is—not religious deities or vanguard heroes—create their gods and their revolutions.

In Western left tradition, we are typically uncomfortable talking about gods, except perhaps in the context of the folkloric. We also often have a narrow definition of revolution. These stories, translated into English with commentaries by the Colectivo Relámpago (Lightning Collective), knock such limitations on their head. As the Colectivo explains more fully throughout, the stories were written between 1992 and 2000, most as part of, or complementary to, communiqués from the Zapatista Army of National Liberation, in a context of fire and blood, in an effort to inform the world about events then unfolding in Chiapas, and to inspire global solidarity as a practical means of gaining support and maybe protection. Each story was thus embedded in the struggle of the present in which it was written. But the struggle had a past, and it has not disappeared with the passage of time and headline news.

That past stretches back thousands of years, to the formation of Mayan culture and the subsequent effort of the people to save their languages and spiritual constructs, camouflaged and altered but not obliterated, after the cataclysm of conquest. The occupiers' history records some organized rebellions since July 11, 1562, when a Spanish Inquisition put thousands of Mayan images and dozens of hieroglyphic codices to the torch in the Yucatán—the word rendered smoke and ash. In neighboring Chiapas and environs, four rebellions (among how many in the lingering present of unrecorded time?) stand out. One hundred fifty years after that auto-de-fe, which, according to its Franciscan supervisor Fr. Diego de Landa, the Maya "regretted to an amazing degree and which caused them great affliction," the Indian Army of the Virgin rose up against the Spanish political and religious powers and principalities. They did not win, but their revolt was remembered. One hundred fifty–some years later, the people's religious iconoclasm and passive resistance to *ladino* economic control in the late 1860s resulted in the massacre of many hundreds of them in San Cristóbal de las Casas, in 1869, and an ethnic/state campaign bent on extermination.

Another century on, in 1974, "radical Tzotziles—the People of the Bat—forced the whites and mestizos off Indian communal lands," as the great journalist John Ross recounted. That same year, at a conference in San Cristóbal celebrating the quincentennial of Bartolomé de las Casas, "the first defender of the Maya," Indigenous people were in charge. In the early 1960s, they had confronted their bishop, Samuel Ruiz, demanding to know whether the Church cared only for heavenly rewards. Ruiz chose humanity. His embrace of liberation theology, with its "preferential option for the poor," prefigured the choice made by a conclave of Latin American bishops in Medellin in the world-shaking year of 1968 and led to the creation of Catholic base communities. Catechists in Chiapas—in particular the women who were their most active members and translators among the six Indigenous language groups in the highlands and jungle—became the cadre along with secular radicals and the largely mestizo band of guerrilla fighters for what would become the most world-shaking Indigenous revolt: the Zapatistas' armed uprising and seizure of San Cristóbal and six other municipal seats on January 1, 1994, in what they call *una guerra contra el olvido*, "a war against oblivion."

Which returns us to these stories. Written as they were in a context of revolt, they are revolutionary documents. Also, and simultaneously, they are literary documents. It is easy to accept the latter, brimming as the stories are with symbolism, metaphor, humor, and conflict, as well as to think of them as entertainment, designed to charm readers and keep them interested, or as a means to whet the appetite, an *amuse bouche* to the really nutritious political meal—tasty but separate. Except that history, the journey of people through time, is no more neatly divisible than are human beings. Plutarch called history a poetess, for good reason.

Timing, technology, and identifying the enemy as a global phenomenon all make the revolt of the *Chiapanecos* since 1994 different from its historical antecedents. Land and freedom were demands of the Indigenous long before Emiliano Zapata made them the slogan of the Mexican Revolution. Autonomy and dignity were the cries of "the people of corn" from the moment the first bearded white man regarded them as subhuman. These four—land, freedom, autonomy, and dignity—are bulwarks against oblivion. The full communiqués detail the exploitation in Chiapas, the Zapatista program against it, and the ruthlessness of the government/paramilitary response: notably, the executions in Ocosingo, in January 1994; the scorched-earth attack, in February 1995; the massacre of civilians in Acteal, in December 1997; the deceit in negotiating peace accords from 1995 to 1997—that last, a feint in the state's overall strategy of extreme violence, which persisted with invasions of Zapatista villages in 1998 and after. The dates are important. The commentaries at the back of the book explain the stories' temporal and political context. They come last so that the reader might first surrender to the imagination, to the surreal.

As in any uprising of the subaltern, when "weapons talk," to borrow Subcomandante Tacho's phrase, they declare, *hear us! see us!* He was speaking of guns, but the widely circulated communiqués were weapons too. Form and content were purposeful. Like freedom dreams, the stories are grounded in their strategic moment at the same time that they transcend it.

They signal a breathtaking revolutionary ambition by reversing the mirror: *see us!/see yourselves!*

Taking the oldest literary forms, the stories assert the stature of the Mayan worldview within the storehouse of human civilization's vast and varied inheritance; in doing so, they reintroduce humanity to itself. And be not deceived, however fanciful the language or whiskered the date, nothing about this project belongs to the curio cupboard. Consider again the nature of the enemy:

> In the new world order there is no democracy, no liberty, no equality, no fraternity.

> In this war of conquest everything and all of us are subjected to the criterion of the market—anything that opposes it or presents an obstacle will be eliminated. It implies the destruction of humanity as a sociocultural collective and reconstructs it as a marketplace. Opposing neoliberalism, fighting against it, is not just one political or ideological option, it is a question of the survival of humanity.

That was Marcos speaking in 1999, in the first instance, to the Spanish writer Manuel Vásquez Montalbán and, in the second, in a 1998 Zapatista communiqué. Both observations condense the Zapatistas' dualistic perspective: yes, their struggle is particular, localized; and, yes, it is global and won't be won by a seizure of state power in this place or that. Nor is the way forward clear cut. "The Story of the Little Mouse and the Little Cat" in this collection involves a struggle over resources between figures of unequal power and position. I'm not spoiling the story by revealing that the resources have all gone bad.

More than two decades after Marcos made the above observations, the exigencies of a pandemic have concentrated political attention on the actions of national governments, but who will argue for the health of democracy, liberty, equality, and fraternity? Who can boast of humanity, when even among leftists there is nonchalance toward mass death?

By the most charitable assessment, we are afraid—and confused. In other words, we are in exactly the position as human beings facing a crisis since time immemorial; we are in the position of our earliest ancestors, trying to know the world and imagine a way forward. Some of us pretend to know perfectly well, but we don't. The wise "walk with questions," like the gods in these stories.

While representing vital elements of ancient tradition, these gods are not replicas. The Zapatistas honor Indigenous history; they don't essentialize it. Like the deities of the *Popol Vuh* (commonly translated as the Book of Counsel), these gods consult, decide, and stumble. Creation is a result of trial and error, of making and remaking. Like the gods of antiquity, who fashioned humans first of mud, then of wood, and finally of corn, these gods are dissatisfied. They must repeatedly confer and come to an agreement again and again. In legend, the mud people could not keep their form and had no understanding. The wooden people could stand and speak but had no soul, no discernment or memory. All of creation participated in destroying them. The people formed out of maize and water were perfect. They knew and understood everything. They could see beyond the dimensions of reality into infinity. They were like their makers, and so the ancient gods, uneasy, adjusted their creation:

> And when they changed the nature of their works, their designs, it was enough that the eyes be marred by the Heart of the Sky. They were blinded as the face of a mirror is breathed upon. Their eyes were weakened. Now it was only when they looked nearby that things were clear.

The story gods show no interest in being worshiped. Plopped into politics, they scratch their stomachs and help blinkered humans learn how to look. They play a ball game (evoking the contest between the Lords of Death and the Hero Twins of the *Popol Vuh*), but it involves language and discernment. They create the animals, who in legend help the Hero Twins outwit death, but who here either represent thought or are marshaled in its service against fear. The ferocious animal is enlisted in parables not to inflate danger—which only reinforces the eternal victim—but to encourage us to take a true measure of it and of our own powers. The lowliest creature teaches the necessity of reason and its attributes; humans must observe, listen, assess, come to an understanding, and be able to laugh at themselves. Fearlessness is not part of the sequence. Humanity is not fearless; it is aware. Change is a constant, and the "sociocultural collective" is a process of creation. It must be made and remade.

The Colectivo invites readers to play, to draw their own interpretations and associations from these stories. Mine spiral out like that symbol for breath, for conversation that enhances thought, for cyclical time. They range from Aesop (who related his song to the cricket's voice and called language "the key to knowledge") to Odysseus (whom animals reprimanded for pomposity) to Ovid's *Metamorphosis* (where "all things change but nothing dies") to the Book of Wisdom ("I too, when born, inhaled the common air and fell onto the kindred earth," says an unknown Jew from Alexandria, writing in Greek, in a time of oppression) to the conscious breath in Hawaiian tradition (and in lovemaking) to Jesus (who returns in a wind to his quaking, immobilized friends and calls them to community) to smoke as the aura of jazz, the incense of Easter, and the ambiance of Rastafari, all the way to popular culture, to *The Book of Eli*, whose blind protagonist, the embodied word, fights his way through dystopia to a remote library, where history can begin again.

If this seems swoony, it might be because we are so unused to thinking of reason and emotion, flesh and spirit, science and art, struggle and living, as complementary aspects of conceptualizing a politics of humanity, for humanity. This collection says, *look again*. One final association on the subject of looking. The famous parable of the men in the dark trying to describe an elephant appears in ancient Hindu, Buddhist, and Jain texts. In every version, no one can perceive the whole; each one is led astray by solitary experience, to explanations of reality that are partial, wildly different, and, thus, no explanation at all. In some versions of the story the men fight or are ridiculed by a king for their ignorance; in others the men are deemed victims of delusion, or they simply decide they're each describing a different animal. Some contemporary interpretations conclude that all is relative, and nothing can be known. The great Sufi poet Rumi had another idea: "If each had a candle and they went in together the differences would disappear." For Rumi, the "sensual eye" is also deceptive, but as the stories here tell, it is not the eye that reveals reality but the act of going in and looking together; and differences, when honestly joined and recognized, do not so much disappear as clarify.

The Zapatistas consider resistance to the culture of death—market hegemony and its violent enforcers—a way of being as much as a way to maneuver. They return politics to the sensuous world. Notice the four images at the end of this book and try to catapult your mind into their cosmic motion, their living color. From the Aztec Codex Borbonicus, the oldest of them, the classic figures are vibrant in red, brown, ochre, green, and indigo. The iconic swirls are brown like the color of the drummer's skin, red seven times from the mouths of the seven figures down the right side, and large and black and white in the upper center of the picture, a swirl containing many swirls. The image from the Codex Florentine, made by Nahua students in central Mexico a generation or so after the conquest, is muted, predominantly white and grey, with swirls like whistles in red and blue. In the first of two Zapatista murals, the soil is brown, the field green, the starry sky deep blue, with a geometric flash of red and pale blue in the upper right corner, from where the black-masked woman stands barefoot and proclaims, dreams, *Autonomía* in a billowy, smoke-like curl of white. The final image, a house mural, is alive with the iconic swirls: yellow-red, like a flame, like the sun, above the family group; aqua and orange spiraling from the masked figures on the right, who stroll by a cornfield on a green mountain under a red star; blue, lilac, and pink among the leaves where two masked Zapatistas pop up at the top of the Tree of Life, anchoring the world and holding up the turquoise sky.

JoAnn Wypijewski

Acknowledgments

This manuscript is the product of a collective process that extended over many years and several geographies, but to which we always returned as if to a home, or, as the Zapatistas would say, to the inside of their and our caracol. This trajectory has been enriched by the contributions of past collective members, including Molly Falsetti-Yu, Hampshire College students Jamie Blair, Dylan Fitzwater, Ellen Green, Wenle Li, and others who brought their knowledge, creativity, and engagement to the undertaking.

Thanks are due to our intimate partners, children, attentive strangers, and readers in solidarity. We are grateful to Marla Erlien, Sofia Erlien-Cerullo, and Aureliano Dunthorn Carcelén for their loving, if exasperated, support over the long time we devoted to this project. We thank Marla especially for continually challenging us to think more critically with probing questions. We are indebted to our careful readers, Yasmin Belkyr, Carol Bengelsdorf, Michelle Bigenho, Velma García, Michelle Joffroy, Sujani Reddy, Stuart Schussler, and JoAnn Wypijewski, whose thoughtful comments enriched the editorial process and greatly improved the manuscript. Mary Watkins and Eduardo Nachman graciously shared with us their photos from Zapatista communities, while Pedro Valtierra, with sympathy for a Zapatista study, has generously made available to our readers his iconic photograph of the Women of X'oyep.

Finally, wonderful librarians Gaby Richard-Harrington and Sika Berger and IT genius Kate MacGregor helped us navigate innumerable quandaries.

To one and all, we extend our thanks.

List of Images

Introduction to the English Translation of *Los Otros Cuentos*

Origin Stories

Since the Zapatistas appeared on the world stage on January 1, 1994, we, along with so many others, have followed with hope and solidarity their unorthodox revolution. We remember our initial surprise at an event that seemed at the very least ill-timed: after the fall of the Soviet Union (1991), after the electoral defeat of the Sandinistas (1990), as the civil wars in El Salvador and Guatemala were winding down—when the time of the guerrilla seemed over—it was then that an army of Indigenous men and women, the Zapatista Army of National Liberation, or EZLN, appeared "from the mountains of the Mexican Southeast" to declare war against the Mexican state. And this, on the very day that the North American Free Trade Agreement (NAFTA) went into effect, marking Mexico's supposed entry into the First World.[1] A few weeks later, writing in the *Nation* magazine, the late, much admired left-wing journalist Andy Kopkind captured with extraordinary lucidity the political earthquake represented by the Zapatistas' appearance:

> [T]he revolt of the Chiapanecos is something stunningly new, the first shots of a rebellion consciously aimed at the new world order, [itself] the dire consequence of a history that did not die as predicted but intrudes in the

most pernicious manner on the way of life of people always overlooked.... It might be that the battle in Chiapas will end with the predictable bangs and whimpers heard whenever outnumbered, outgunned peasants without powerful international support are picked off and packed away. But the shots fired in Mexico in the first week of the new year have been heard around the world, and their echoes will not soon stop.[2]

No less unexpected was the EZLN's idiosyncratic spokesperson who answered with humor the worried question of a tourist trapped in a war in San Cristóbal de las Casas: "Excuse the inconvenience, but this is a revolution."[3] Yet, of course, beyond the humor of Subcomandante Marcos, he and all the EZLN were fully aware of their precarious situation. To take up arms, as they did, against a national army that could easily have annihilated them revealed the urgency in the rebels' cry of *¡Ya Basta!* (Enough Is Enough!). We would later come to understand that the 1992 revision of the Mexican Constitution, a condition for Mexico's entry into NAFTA, was, for the Indigenous peoples, a death sentence. It brought agrarian reform to an end, spelling the defeat of a centuries-long Indigenous struggle to recuperate their land—and, with it, recover place, identity, and power. Immediately, the change in the law awakened a visceral fear: the return to the plantation economy of the fincas where their parents and grandparents, and some of the insurgent commanders themselves, had been virtually enslaved.[4] NAFTA, for its part, is a centerpiece of neoliberalism, the post–Cold War, US-led new world order. Its defining features are the shrinking of the welfare state, the privatization of everything (health, education, welfare, natural resources), along with "open borders" for goods from the US and other great powers, while the movement of people, many of them displaced by neoliberal policies, is policed and restricted. Promising to "lift every boat," the results of neoliberal policies globally have been instead an enormous transfer of wealth (resources, land, labor) from the poor to the rich.[5]

A World in Which Many Worlds Fit

Mexican civil society responded to the Zapatista cry of ¡Ya Basta! by taking to the streets to demand that the government stop what was in effect a war of elimination and negotiate. Civil society prevailed. Up to a point. Since that moment, while fending off paramilitary attacks, as well as near constant military incursions into their communities, the Zapatistas have not only survived for more than twenty-five years without being annihilated; they have continued to evolve, demonstrating a remarkable inventiveness and flexibility, all the while trying to make links to others in their "war against oblivion." They have worked to strengthen a global anti-capitalist movement and to share their efforts to create, in their words, "a world where many worlds fit."

This is not merely a turn of phrase. The Zapatista priority of "making space for difference," as in their demand on the Mexican state that they want to be Mexican without ceasing to be Indigenous, which has distinguished them. This is a notion of inclusion, in this case, a notion of citizenship that recognizes equality *and* difference.[6] The Zapatistas are also distinctive in their open embrace of the many differences that have so often undone the left—not only of ethnicity and race but of sexuality and gender. Throughout their public history, they have sought spaces of *encuentro*—encounter and dialogue. In fact, dialogue or the dialogic relation is at the heart of Zapatismo. The first critical encounter, in the 1970s and 1980s, was the meeting of mestizo guerrillas of the Fuerzas de Liberación Nacional (FLN) from the north of Mexico with local Indigenous militants in Chiapas that resulted in dethroning the classic Marxist-Leninist guerrilla—vanguardist, top-down, ideologically rigid[7]—and the emergence of a new, now *Indianized*, vision of revolution.[8] The FLN leadership was replaced by the more democratic General Command of the Indigenous Revolutionary Clandestine Committee (CCRI-CG), characterized by two distinctive traits: their tradition of extensive consultation with their communities before taking major decisions;[9] and their practice of open-ended questioning at each turn of action, *caminar preguntando* (we walk with questions), based on the insistence that the path forward cannot be fixed in advance but is shaped by those one encounters in struggle along the way. This framework, dependent as it is engaging, strengthening, and learning from the struggles of others "from below and to the left," has prompted the Zapatistas to convene multiple encuentros in Chiapas, proposing to discuss with all those interested, be they Mexicans, internationals, or *intergalactic* visitors, about how to break the limited conception of democracy that condemns populations to invisibility, their cultural memory to oblivion, and their needs and knowledge to subaltern status.

They have repeatedly signaled that their abandonment and dire economic circumstances are not exclusive to them as Indigenous but are common to many other Mexicans, urban and rural, as well as dispossessed and excluded people everywhere. Their solidarity and appeal, as well as their creativity and steadfastness, summoned all those in all the continents who aspire to a more just and inclusive society. This desire for encounter and dialogue continues into the current moment, with their latest initiative, the first leg of a five-continent expedition to meet and learn from other struggles "for life and against capitalism," which we discuss below.[10]

Reinventing Politics: The Other Campaign (2006), the Silent March (2012), the Little School (2013–2014), the National Indigenous Congress (CNI) (1996–present)

Throughout nearly thirty years of public life, the Zapatistas have continued to surprise with their constant efforts to reinvent radical politics. Some highlights include the 2006 "Other

Campaign," a national "listening tour" to coincide with the time of the Mexican presidential election, when all eyes were focused on politics. Instead of coming to the people with plans and proposals of candidates and parties, the Zapatista *Delegate Zero*, one of Subcomandante Marcos's personas, visited communities from Yucatán to the northern border to learn about and from the struggles Mexicans were waging "against neoliberalism and for humanity." The listening tour, in fact, revealed in detail the incursions of an ever more predatory, savage, relentless capitalism that seems to have its sights set on every uncommodified waterfront, forest, spring, and plant in the country.[11] The Other Campaign in turn had been launched with the publication of the "Sixth Declaration of the Lacandon Jungle" (known as the "Sexta," or "Sixth"), in July 2005, a document that elaborates in remarkably accessible language the Zapatistas' anti-capitalist vision of the world.[12]

Following the Other Campaign, and after several years of silence, the Zapatistas returned to the public stage on December 21, 2012, the day of the supposed "end of the world" according to the Mayan calendar, with a Silent March.[13] On that day, forty-five thousand Zapatistas (women, babies, children, men) walked in disquieting silence into and out of San Cristóbal de las Casas and three other towns they had taken in 1994, Ocosingo, Las Margaritas, and Altamirano, as well as Palenque, later issuing a communiqué that said: "Did you hear? That is the sound of your world crumbling, and of ours resurging."

Continuing to experiment and to engage supporters, a year after the Silent March, the Zapatistas invited the world to come to Chiapas to participate in an *Escuelita* (Little School), to learn, not in the classroom but from Zapatista families and communities, what "autonomy according to the Zapatistas" means in practice. Some three thousand did indeed turn up, for three sessions in August and December 2013 and in January 2014.[14]

Since 1996, the Zapatistas have also worked to forge a collective Indigenous political identity by convening the National Indigenous Congress (CNI) to participate in their negotiations with the government over Indigenous rights, since those negotiations had implications for all Indigenous peoples in Mexico. The CNI was revived in recent years and, in 2017, again took advantage of the electoral season as the Zapatistas had done eleven years earlier. This time they ran an Indigenous woman and CNI founding member, María de Jesús Patricio Martínez, known as Marichuy, from Jalisco, Guadalajara, as their presidential candidate.[15] Despite discriminatory technological obstacles that made it impossible for her independent candidacy to succeed, Marichuy's cause, according to Juan Villoro, "acquired enormous visibility not only among the Indigenous but within the digital generation" (for example, in one month her Facebook page had 450,000 visits).[16] In any case, her candidacy was not about seeking power as granted through parties and elections. In the aftermath of the brutal disappearance of forty-three mostly Indigenous students from the Ayotzinapa teacher-training school,[17] and in the face of escalating violence throughout the country, the CNI and the Zapatistas did not seek state power but, rather, aimed to foster organizing and to expand alternative projects to counter the crisis in Indigenous communities.

Resistance as a Way of Life: The Zapatistas' Autonomy Project

When their efforts to negotiate with the government for a more inclusive state and society had decisively failed, the Zapatistas pivoted and, in 2003, announced to the world the formal creation of five new autonomous regions or caracoles. This was now not a negotiation but a de facto decision. As Comandante Brus Li put it at the time, "We must organize ourselves as true rebels and not wait for someone to give us permission to be autonomous."[18]

The Zapatista designation of their new autonomous region as "caracoles" literally references the conch shell used to convoke communal assemblies since pre-Columbian times. In "Chiapas the Thirteen Stele, Part 1: A *Caracol*," Subcomandante Marcos elaborates some of the multiple meanings of the caracol: "People here say … that the first people in these lands valued the shape of the conch … they say that the conch represents entering into the heart, which is how the first ones described knowledge…and they say that the conch also represents going out from the heart … into the world, which is what the first ones called life. And, not only that, they say … that with the conch you summon the community so that the word can flow from one to another and an agreement be born. And they also say that the conch helped the era hear even the most distant of words."[19]

These five caracoles would coordinate the already existing Zapatista municipalities in rebellion. The latter, created in 1994, were based on their massive land seizures during the uprising.[20] Those municipalities would now be governed not by the EZLN command, with its vertical military structure, but by civilian good governance councils (*juntas de buen gobierno*).

The transformation of the internal life of the communities within the framework of de facto autonomy has perhaps been the most remarkable development of the years since then, as the Zapatista project has become an ongoing cultural revolution. An act of rebellion transformed itself into a way of living, Mariana Mora argues, redefining the meaning of resistance (and revolution): "rather than a suspended moment, liberated when transformation arrives so the collective can rest or lower their guard, [resistance] is itself a form of living that reaches out to the apparently unattainable … horizon of social justice."[21] The occupation of land, its re-inscription with Indigenous identity, and an anti-capitalist logic through the development of collective priorities: sustainable and equitable economies, community schools and health clinics, the use of Indigenous languages, distinctive practices of justice, participatory self-government—all this is the exercise of autonomy. For the Zapatistas, then, autonomy becomes a "perpetual act of negating particular imposed ways of being"— from racist colonial legacies that cast Indigenous bodies as scenery, today, as colorful attractions for tourists, through the state's offer of social programs that foster dependence and division within the communities to neoliberal projects of dispossession and displacement, such as the vaunted "Mayan Train" of the current self-identified leftist Mexican administration.[22] And, in the case of Zapatista women, autonomy involves resistance to patriarchal social expectations, including those of their families and communities.

The Revolution of the Women

The propulsive force of autonomy has again and again been women. According to Marcos, during the years of clandestine organizing, it was Indigenous women who insistently spread the idea that became a refrain throughout the highlands and jungle of Chiapas: "¡Ya Basta!"—something had to be done to forestall the death worlds that the Indigenous inhabited. Women were a strong presence in the Zapatista guerrilla, a third of the Zapatista army. This is notable since Indigenous women in Chiapas led extremely restricted lives before they were recruited into the Zapatista army. Beyond those exemplary soldiers and comandantas who embodied for women in the communities a new way of being, an imagination of freedom, women became and have remained central to the Zapatista support bases. Their militance in facing off with soldiers has become iconic in the representation of the movement—see, for example, the Women of X'oyep, discussed in our commentary to "The Story of the Lion and the Mirror" below. From documents, such as the film El Corazón del Tiempo (2009), made in collaboration with a Zapatista community,[23] our own visits to Zapatista communities,[24] and the careful work of feminist activist anthropologists,[25] we have been able to catch a glimpse of the politics that women have continuously engaged in, challenging the power relations of everyday life in the communities, from arranged marriage to the division of labor, from control over reproduction to the locus of political decision-making.

The proclamation of the Women's Revolutionary Law, before the 1994 uprising, was an insistence that women's rights cannot wait until after the revolution; they are part of the revolution. If the Revolutionary Law is an articulation of women's rights, it is the practice of autonomy that has made those rights concrete and extended their meanings. Zapatista women, for example, have articulated the right to bodily autonomy, reclaiming the territory of their bodies, collectively inscribing them with new possibilities—these are bodies that play basketball and sometimes abandon *traje* (the traditional dress of heavy woolen skirts and embroidered blouses) for more comfortable and mobile blue jeans. They are women who will take into their own hands the determination of how many children to have—in the words of one young Zapatista, *sin pedir permiso del estado* (without asking permission from the state), even when abortion is illegal, linking the autonomy of their bodies with the autonomy of their communities. They have articulated a distinctive Zapatista feminism, a body politics that links the multiple powers they contend with as Indigenous women— from enduring colonial legacies to the *mal gobierno*, from neoliberalism to the patriarchal structures of communities.

The Right to Drive

In 2018 and 2019, Zapatista women organized international women's encuentros that brought as many as eight thousand women to Chiapas to join two thousand Zapatistas.[26] In their preparations for these meetings, young Zapatista women learned to drive the trucks that transported visitors and supplies to provision the encuentros. According to Marcos/ Galeano,[27] one of the little-known provisions of the 1993

Revolutionary Women's Law was the right to drive, which, nearly thirty years later, Zapatista women enacted. Recalling the 1970s US Women's Liberation Movement,[28] Zapatista women have also been learning auto mechanics, so that they can fully take charge of transportation without suffering condescending dependence on men.[29] The Zapatista women also joined the feminist strike on March 8, 2020,[30] a transnational feminist "political invention" that has become a principal way of calling angry attention to multiple forms of violence against women, up to and including femicide (systematic murder of women) throughout Latin America and in Eastern Europe.[31]

Reversing the Conquest

As we mentioned above, in the spring of 2021, the Zapatistas launched their most daring initiative to date—a five-continent expedition of learning and solidarity. Beginning with a sea voyage to Europe (reversing the voyage of the Spanish conquest of Tenochtitlan in 1521), they will visit collectives all over the European continent, returning the extraordinary solidarity that Europeans have shown them over the years, and revealing to many of us an-"other" Europe, below and to the left.[32] As we write this, the first small group arrived in Vigo, Basque Country, Spain, where Marijose, a trans woman, turning history upside down, proclaimed with characteristic Zapatista humor and seriousness:

> In the name of the Zapatista women, children, men, elderly, and, of course, others, I declare that from now on this place, currently referred to as "Europe" by those who live here, be called: SLUMIL K´AJXEMK´OP, which means "Rebellious Land" or "Land which does not give in or give up." And that is how it will be known by its own people and by others for as long as there is at least someone here who does not surrender, sell out, or give up.[33]

Final Note on the Stories That Follow and on Translating Zapatismo

In 2008, the Zapatista Secondary School in Oventic proposed the publication of a group of Subcomandante Marcos's stories to the Argentine Zapatista Solidarity Network. The resulting collection, *Los Otros Cuentos*,[34] included twelve stories that they selected together. It was published that year by the Cooperativa Imprenta Chilavert, a press "recuperated" by its workers during the 2002 Argentine financial crisis.[35] This original anthology was taken up by collectives in other countries, who translated it into German (2010), Norwegian (2012), French (2014), and Italian (2016). Our collective formed to create an English-language version of *Los Otros Cuentos*. The stories gathered here are, therefore, by no means a Zapatista canon but, rather, an accidental archive of the Zapatista struggle that emerged from international solidarity networks. Who is their author? Subcomandante Marcos penned all of them, always telling us which were told to him by "Old Antonio," who he tells us was a real person, not a literary creation,[36] which were by Durito, a scholarly beetle and Marcos alter ego, and which are his own.

Initially, we intended simply to translate the stories but found that investigating their context recast them as political interventions. Translation turned into dialogue as we speculated on their possible links with the past or their anticipations of a future in what was, and remains, an ongoing open-ended revolution. Our commentaries try to capture the stories' transdisciplinary character: they are literature, history, philosophy, cultural studies. To grasp their richness, you need to know politics, Chiapas and national (not to mention Latin American) history, economics, sociology, even ethnography. Sprinkled throughout writings that are driven by engagement with Mexican politics and the world's neoliberal transformations are references to writers like Federico García Lorca, Jorge Luis Borges, Miguel Hernández, William Shakespeare, and Bertolt

Brecht—the latter in conversation with the beetle Don Durito de la Lacandona at Café Comandanta Ramona in Mexico City, where Marcos listens in as a waiter. Other characters featured include those from US cartoons, like Speedy Gonzalez or the Cat-Dog, or Mayan historical and spiritual figures, such as the hybrid cultural hero Votán-Zapata (like the writers mentioned above, all men as far as we can tell). In other words, great writers of modernity, popular cartoons, Mayan and Mexican history, and many others.

Our process has amounted to an archeological digging, uncovering layers of sedimented meaning, which we try to make visible for the reader with our commentaries. At times, we thought we understood something to then discover that we didn't. We would set off in pursuit of one thing and end up with something entirely different. For example, the figure of "Nebuchadnezzar" appears in the first Durito story in this collection as one of the beetle's personas. We went off to clarify this biblical referent: a great warrior, the Chaldean king, conqueror of Jerusalem who enslaved the Jews. Then, we remembered Rubén Darío's poem "To Teddy Roosevelt,"[37] written in 1904 after the US takeover of Panama. Darío casts Roosevelt as Alexander-Nebuchadnezzar (combining the imperial Alexander the Great with the destroyer of Jerusalem). For some Latin American readers, and probably for poetry-loving Marcos, the first association to Nebuchadnezzar would likely be its use in this poem, an allusion to an ancient warrior-king to highlight the power of a modern ruler. The allusion here creates humorous contrast and not similarity. In the end, we wondered if Nebuchadnezzar is just a very big name for a tiny beetle—pompous and fancy.

An excursus about the number seven is another example of this narrative labyrinth. Seven, presumably Mayan, gods, the first ones, gave birth to the world. They populate many of these stories. We all know seven is some sort of magic number. But we found a text where Comandante Tacho, handing the *bastón de mando* (staff, symbol of authority) to Marcos, says: "Seven forces: tzotzil, tzeltal, tojolabal, chol, mame, zoque, and mestizo let the struggle grow seven times over. Seven words and seven paths: life, truth, humanity, peace, democracy, freedom, and justice. Seven paths that give force to the bastón de mando of the commander of the true men and women."[38]

So it turns out this is not only figurative language but coded language. If you don't know the code, you're satisfied with the metaphor (magic numbers or biblical figures) but you most likely will miss the invocation of those seven members of distinct ethnic groups who came together to found the EZLN, those first gods, those who gave birth to (this new) world. The Zapatista communiqués preceding the 2021 European voyage told us that the advance guard of this expedition would consist of seven Zapatistas. By now we know the code, or most of it, but read on. The Sup asks, "Why only seven? Well, we could talk about the seven cardinal points, or the seven first gods, those who gave birth to the world, etc. But the truth is that, far from symbols and allegories, the number is due to the fact that the majority still haven't been able to get passports; we are still in that struggle." Besides, there weren't a ton of eager volunteers to undertake a possibly treacherous voyage on the high seas.

A final example below. In one of our commentaries, we talk about "the heart" as a significant motif and elaborate on it.[39] But we have since read (or reread) that, for the Tojolabales, thinking occurs in the heart. "When they want to say 'I think,' they say: 'My heart says.'" We have left our original commentary as is. The reader can always play.[40]

Los hombres y mujeres verdaderos invite us to dream with them but follow our own path to autonomy. This invitation has been taken up by Kurdish and Kichwa alike, across continents, in translation. The indeterminacy of the Zapatista future, the open horizon of justice, the possibility of everything, is what makes Zapatismo so useful for many around the world oppressed by the neoliberal war against humanity.

As we come to the end of our project, we hope our commentaries communicate how much we have learned. We wish to underline here how much we still don't know. Thus, our commentaries are meant to be an invitation to others to shake loose different, even contrary, meanings as you walk your own path into Zapatismo and autonomy.

The Stories

Antonio Dreams
August 1992

Antonio dreams that the land he works belongs to him. He dreams his sweat earns him justice and truth. He dreams of schools that cure ignorance and medicine that frightens away death. He dreams his house has light and his table is full, his land is free, and his people have the right to govern and self-govern. He dreams he is at peace with himself and with the world.

He dreams he must fight to have this dream. He dreams there must be death for there to be life.

Antonio dreams, and he awakens...

Now he knows what to do: he sees his wife kneeling to stoke the fire, hears his child crying, looks at the sun greeting them from the east, and sharpens his machete, smiling.

A wind rises and everything is turned on its head. Antonio stands and walks to meet others. Something tells him that his dream is shared by many, and he goes looking for them.

The viceroy dreams that his realm is shaken by a terrible wind that turns everything upside down. He dreams that what he has stolen is taken back. He dreams his house is destroyed and the kingdom he rules is crumbling,

He dreams and does not sleep.

The viceroy goes to the feudal lords, and they tell him that they too have these dreams. The viceroy can't rest, he goes to his doctors, and they all agree that this must be Indian witchcraft, they all agree that only blood will free the viceroy from this spell. He orders killings and imprisonments and builds more jails and barracks, but this dream still keeps him awake at night.

In this country, everyone dreams. Now the time has come to wake up.

THE STORM…

…is upon us.

It will be born of the collision of these two winds, its time has come, the furnace of history is ready to burn… Now the wind from above reigns, but the one from below is coming, the storm rises… So it will be.

THE PROPHECY…

…is upon us.

When the storm subsides, when the rain and the fire leave the earth again in peace, the world will no longer be the world, but something better.

Durito's Story
April 10, 1994

Let me tell you a story about something that happened to me the other day. It's the story of a little beetle who wears glasses and smokes a pipe. I met him one day when I was looking for my tobacco and couldn't find it. All of a sudden, I saw to the side of my hammock that a little tobacco had fallen and was forming a thin trail. I followed it to figure out where my tobacco had gone and who the hell had taken it and was spilling it. A few meters away behind a rock, I found a beetle sitting at a little desk, reading some papers, and smoking a tiny pipe.

"Ahem, ahem," I said so that the beetle would take note of my presence, but he paid no attention.

So I said to him, "Hey, that tobacco is mine."

The beetle took off his glasses, looked me over from top to bottom, and said very angrily, "Please, Captain, I beg you not to interrupt me. Can't you see I'm studying?"

I was taken aback and was going to kick him out of the way, but then I calmed down and sat nearby to wait until he finished studying. After a while, he gathered his papers, put them away in his desk, and, chewing his pipe, he said, "Very well, then, how can I be of service to you, Captain?"

"My tobacco," I answered.

"Your tobacco?" he said. "Would you like some?"

I started to get angry, but the little beetle passed me the bag of tobacco with his tiny leg as he added, "Don't get angry,

4

Captain. You need to understand that it's impossible to get tobacco around here, and I had to take some of yours."

I calmed down. I was beginning to like the beetle, so I told him, "Don't worry. I have more back there."

"Mmmh," he answered.

"What is your name, sir?" I asked him.

"Nebuchadnezzar," he said, and continued, "but my friends call me Durito.* You may call me Durito, Captain."

I thanked him for the honor and asked him what it was that he was studying.

"I am studying neoliberalism and its strategy to dominate Latin America," he answered.

"What use is that to a beetle?" I asked him.

He responded very angrily, "What do you mean, what use? I have to know how long this fight of yours is going to last, and whether or not you are going to win. Besides, a beetle should care enough to study the situation of the world he lives in. Don't you agree, Captain?"

"I don't know," I said. "Why do you want to know how long our fight is going to last and whether we're going to win or not?"

"Clearly you haven't understood a thing," he replied, putting on his glasses and lighting his pipe. After blowing a mouthful of smoke, he continued, "It's in order to know how long we beetles need to be on the lookout so that you don't squash us with your enormous boots."

"Ah!" I said.

"Mmh," he said.

"And what conclusion have you reached in your study?" I asked him.

---

* Nebuchadnezzar appears to be a reference to the biblical character—who reappears in Rubén Darío, "To Roosevelt" (1904), accessed October 3, 2021, https://tinyurl.com/533wbbt7. *Durito* means *tough little one.*

He took his papers from his desk and began leafing through them. "Hmm... mhm," he said every so often as he looked them over.

When he had finished, he looked me in the eye and said,

"You are going to win."

"I already knew that," I said. And I added, "But how long is it going to take?"

"A long time," he told me, sighing with resignation.

"I knew that already, too... You don't know exactly how long, do you?" I asked.

"One cannot know exactly. One has to take into account many things: the objective conditions, the maturity of the subjective conditions, the correlation of forces, the crisis of imperialism, the crisis of socialism, etc., etc."

"Mmh," I said.

"What are you thinking about, Captain?"

"Nothing," I answered. "Very well, Señor Durito, I have to go. It was a pleasure meeting you. Please feel free to take as much tobacco as you want, whenever you want."

"Thank you, Captain. And there is no need to call me Señor."

"Thank you, Durito. I will tell my troops that from now on it is forbidden to step on beetles. I hope that helps."

"Thank you, Captain. That will be very helpful."

"In any case, you should still be careful, because my men are very absent-minded, and they don't always pay attention to where they put their feet."

"Understood, Captain."

"See you soon."

"See you. Come whenever you want, and we can talk."

"I'll do that," I said and returned to headquarters.

The Lion Kills by Looking
August 24, 1994

Old Antonio hunted a mountain lion with his ancient shotgun. I had made fun of his weapon just days before: "They were using weapons like that when Hernán Cortés conquered Mexico," I had said to him. He defended himself: "Sure, but look who's wielding it now." Now he is taking the last shreds of flesh from the hide to tan it. He proudly shows me the hide. It doesn't have a single hole in it. "Right in the eye," he boasts. "That's the only way to keep the hide intact." "What are you going to do with it?" I ask. Old Antonio does not answer. He continues scraping the hide with his machete in silence. I sit down next to him and after filling my pipe attempt to roll him a corn husk cigarette. I silently offer it to him. He examines it and takes it apart. "You're not there yet," he tells me, as he rerolls it. We sit down and begin the ceremony of smoking together.

Between puffs, Old Antonio spins the story.

"The lion is strong because the other animals are weak. The lion eats their flesh, because they allow him to eat it. The lion does not kill with claws or fangs. The lion kills by looking.

"First, he approaches slowly—in silence, because he has clouds on his paws that dampen the noise. Next, he pounces and, with a swipe, takes his victim down, more by surprise than by force. After that, he just stares at his prey. The lion looks at his prey like this..." Old Antonio furrows his brow and fixes his black eyes on me. "The poor little animal who is going to die just stares: all it can do is look at the lion looking at it. The little animal no longer sees itself. It sees what the lion sees. It sees the image of a little animal, and in that gaze it is small and weak. Before this, the little animal had never thought about whether or not it was small or weak; it was just a little animal, neither big nor small, neither strong nor weak. But, now, seeing itself in the eyes of the lion, it sees fear. And, seeing how it appears to the lion, the little animal, all on its own, convinces itself that it is small and weak. And seeing the fear that the lion sees, it is afraid. Then the little animal stops looking at anything, and its bones become numb, like when we get caught in the rain in the mountains, in the night, in the cold. And the little animal surrenders, gives up, and the lion gobbles it down, just like that. This is how the lion kills. He kills by looking.

"But there is one little animal that doesn't respond in this way. When he comes across the lion, he ignores him and continues as usual. If the lion swipes at him, he answers by clawing with his hands, which may be tiny, but the blood they draw certainly hurts. This little animal does not back down, because he does not see the lion staring at him. He is blind. 'Mole' is what they call this little animal."

Old Antonio seems to have finished talking. I venture a "Yes, but..."
Old Antonio doesn't let me finish and continues telling the story
while he rolls another cigarette. He does it slowly, turning to look
at me every so often to make sure I am still paying attention.

"The mole went blind because, instead of looking outward, he began to look into his heart; he insisted on looking inward. No one knows how this idea of looking inward got into the mole's head. The mole was so stubborn about looking into his heart that he didn't worry about things like strong or weak, big or small, because the heart is the heart, and it isn't measured the way things and animals are. However, it so happens that only the gods were permitted to look inward, so they punished the mole and didn't allow him to look outward anymore. Even worse, they condemned him to live and crawl under the earth. That's why the mole lives underground, because the gods punished him. But the mole wasn't even upset, since he continued looking inward.

"That's why the mole is not afraid of the lion. Neither is the man who knows how to look into his heart. Because the man who knows how to look into his heart does not see the strength of the lion, what he sees is the strength of his heart, and then he looks at the lion who sees the man looking at him. There, in the man's gaze, the lion sees that he is a mere lion and sees himself being stared at, and he is afraid and runs away."

"So did you look into your heart to kill this lion?" I interrupt. "Me?" he answers." "No way! I concentrated on where the gun was aimed and where the lion's eye was and fired, just like that. My heart didn't even cross my mind." I scratch my head the way they do around here whenever they don't understand something. Old Antonio stands up slowly. He takes the hide and examines it carefully. Then he rolls it up and hands it to me. "Take it," he says. "It's for you so that you never forget that the lion and fear are both killed by knowing where to look."

Old Antonio turns around and goes inside his home. In Old Antonio's language, that means: "I'm done. Adiós." I put the hide of the lion in my nylon bag and leave...

The Story of the Little
Mouse and the Little Cat
August 7, 1995

Once upon a time, there was a little mouse who was very hungry and wanted to eat a little bit of cheese that was in the little kitchen of the little house. So the little mouse marched right up to the little kitchen to grab the little bit of cheese, but, as it happened, a little cat appeared in front of him, and the little mouse got very frightened and ran away and couldn't get to the little bit of cheese in the little kitchen.

So the little mouse thought for some time about how to get the little bit of cheese in the little kitchen, and he came up with this: "I know—I'll put out a little saucer of milk, and the little cat will drink it right up, because little cats really like milk. And then when the little cat is drinking his little saucer of milk and isn't paying attention, I'll go to the little kitchen and grab the little bit of cheese and gobble it down. What a greeeat idea!" gloated the little mouse.

So the little mouse left to go look for a little bit of milk, but, as it happened, the milk was in the little kitchen, and when the little mouse tried to go to the little kitchen, the little cat appeared in front of him, and the little mouse got very frightened and ran away and couldn't get to the milk.

The little mouse thought for some time about how he could get the milk in the little kitchen, and he came up with this: "I know—I'll throw a little bit of fish really far away, and the little cat will run to eat the little fish, because little cats really like eating little fish. Then when the little cat is eating his little fish and isn't paying attention, I'll go to the little kitchen and get the milk and put it in the little saucer, and when the little cat is drinking the milk and isn't paying attention, I'll go to the little kitchen and grab the little bit of cheese and gobble it down. What a greeeat idea!" gloated the little mouse.

So the little mouse went to look for a little fish, but, as it happened, the fish was in the little kitchen, and when the little mouse tried to go to the little kitchen, the little cat appeared in front of him, and the little mouse got very frightened and ran away and couldn't get to the little fish. And so the little mouse saw that the little cheese he wanted, the milk, and the little fish were all in the little kitchen, and he couldn't get there, because the little cat wouldn't let him.

And so the little mouse said, "¡Ya basta! Enough!" and grabbed a machine gun and riddled the little cat with bullets and hurried to the little kitchen and found that the fish, the milk, and the cheese had all gone bad and could no longer be eaten. The little mouse then went back to where the little cat was lying and chopped up his body and made a huge barbecue, and then invited over all of his little friends, and they had a party and ate barbecued cat and sang and danced and lived very happily. That is when history began.

This is the end of our fable and the end of this missive. I remind you that divisions between countries serve only to define the crime of contraband and to justify wars.

Indeed, there exist at least two things that transcend borders: one is the crime disguised as modernity that distributes misery on a global scale; the other is the hope that shame will exist only when someone misses a dance step, and not every time we look at ourselves in the mirror. To bring an end to the crime and make hope bloom, we need only to struggle and to become better. The rest falls into place on its own and is what fills libraries and museums.

Conquering the whole world isn't necessary; it is enough to make it anew... Cheers, and know that for love, a bed is only a pretext; for dancing, a tune is only embellishment; and for struggle, nationality is merely an accident of circumstance.

From the mountains of the Mexican Southeast,
Don Durito de la Lacandona

The Story of the Sword, the Tree, the Stone, and the Water
September 29, 1995

That reminds me of something Old Antonio said when he blew on the fire to revive with it his memories. In this way, between past and present insurgencies, between the encounter of smoke and fire, as when one puts down a valuable but heavy load, Old Antonio unburdened himself of the words that narrated...

"The Story of the Sword, the Tree, the Stone, and the Water"

Old Antonio chews on his pipe. He chews on his words and gives them shape and meaning. Old Antonio speaks, the rain stops to listen, the water subsides, and the darkness brings a respite.

"The greatest of our ancestors had to fight the strangers who came to conquer these lands. They came to impose on us a different way of life, a different word, a different belief, a different god, a different justice. Their justice functioned only to give to them and take from us. Gold was their god. Superiority their belief. Deceit their word. Cruelty their way.

"Our people, our greatest warriors, confronted them. Great and terrible battles were fought by the native people to defend these lands from the grasp of the stranger, but also great was the force of the stranger's hand. Strong and noble warriors fell and died in combat. The battles raged on, few warriors remained, and women and children took up the arms of those who had fallen.

"It was then that the wisest of our ancestors assembled and told the story of the sword, the tree, the stone, and the water. They said that long, long ago, up in the mountains, the things that men used for work and to defend themselves met together.

"The gods were walking around the way they used to, that is to say, half-asleep, because at that time the gods were very lazy—these were not the greatest gods, not the ones who gave birth to the world, not the first ones. Meanwhile, in some corner of the dawn, a man and woman were tiring their bodies and livening their hearts. The night, for her part, was silent, aware of how little time she had left. It was then that the sword spoke.

"A sword like this one," Old Antonio interrupts himself and brandishes a giant double-edged machete. For a fleeting instant, the firelight catches the blade. Then darkness returns. Old Antonio continues, "Then the sword spoke and said: 'I am the strongest and I can destroy everyone. My blade is sharp and I give power to whoever wields me and death to whoever defies me.' 'Lies!' said the tree, 'I am the strongest. I have resisted the wind and the fiercest of storms.' The sword and the tree fought. The tree stood strong and hard and faced the sword. The sword swung, struck, and struck again until it cut through the trunk and toppled the tree. 'I am the strongest,' the sword said once again.

"'Lies!' said the stone. 'I am the strongest, because I am hard and ancient, dense and heavy.' And now the sword and the stone fought. The stone stood hard and firm and faced the sword. The sword swung, struck, and struck again, but couldn't destroy the stone, though it broke it into many pieces. The sword wound up dull, and the stone shattered. 'It's a tie!' said the sword and the stone, and they both cried at the vainglory of their fight.

"Meanwhile, the water of the stream simply watched the fight and said nothing. The sword looked at the water and said,

'You are the weakest of all. You can't do anything to anyone. I am stronger than you!' So the sword flung itself with great force at the water of the stream. There followed a big scene and a great deal of noise, the fish were frightened, and the water did not resist the blows of the sword. Little by little, without saying a thing, the water regained its shape, enveloped the sword, and continued on its path to the river, which would carry it to the great waters that the gods had created to quench their thirst.

"Time passed, and there in the water, the sword began to turn old and rusty. It lost its sharpness, and the fish would approach without fear and make fun of it. Ashamed, the sword withdrew itself from the water of the stream. Now blunt and defeated, the sword complained: 'I am stronger than the water, but I can't hurt her, while she, without fighting, has defeated me!' The dawn passed and the sun came to awaken the man and woman who, together, had become exhausted making each other new. The man and woman found the sword in a dark corner, the stone broken into pieces, the tree fallen, and the water of the stream, singing...

"The ancestors finished telling themselves the story of the sword, the tree, the stone, and the water and said to one another: 'There are times when we must fight like a sword confronting an animal; there are times when we have to fight like a tree weathering a storm; there are times when we have to fight like a stone against time. But there are times when we must fight like the water against the sword, the tree, and the stone. This is the time to become water and follow our path toward a river, which will take us to the great waters where the great gods, those who gave birth to the world, the first ones, quench their thirst.'

"And that is what our ancestors did," Old Antonio says. "They resisted as water resists the fiercest blows. The strangers came with their strength, scared the weak, thought they had won, and with time became old and rusty. The strangers ended up in a corner, ashamed, without understanding why, even though they had won, they were lost."

Old Antonio relights his pipe and then the logs of the fire and adds: "This was how our greatest and wisest ancestors won the great war against the strangers.

"The strangers went away. We are still here. Like the water of the stream, we continue to walk toward the river that will carry us to the vast waters where the greatest gods, those who gave birth to the world, the first ones, quench their thirst."

The dawn melted away and, with it, Old Antonio. I followed the path of the sun westward along a stream that snaked toward the river. In front of the mirror between the rising sun and the setting sun is the tender caress of the midnight sun. A relief that is a wound; water that is thirst; an encounter that remains a quest...

One February, just like the sword from Old Antonio's story, the government's offensive entered Zapatista land without any difficulty. Powerful, dazzling, and with a resplendent hilt, the sword of power struck Zapatista territory.

Like the sword in Old Antonio's story, the government's offensive made a scene and a great deal of noise, and like the sword it scared some fish. Just as in Old Antonio's story, its blow was great, strong... and in vain.

Like the sword in Old Antonio's story, the government's offensive continues to rust and age in the water. And the water? It follows its path, envelops the sword, and paying it no heed reaches the river that will carry it to the great water where the greatest gods, those who gave birth to the world, the first ones, quench their thirst...

The Story of Noise and Silence
February 14, 1997

"There was a time long ago when time was not measured. In that time the greatest gods, those who gave birth to the world, walked in the way that first gods do, that is, they danced. In that time there was a lot of noise, and you could hear voices and shouting all over the place. A lot of noise, and none of it made sense. And that's because the purpose of the noise was not to understand anything but to make sure nothing would be understood. At first, the gods believed that the noise was music, and so quickly they grabbed their partners and began to dance, like this"—Old Antonio gets to his feet and attempts a dance step that consists of balancing himself first on one foot, then on the other. "It turns out that the noise was neither music nor dance, it was just plain noise; you couldn't dance to it and be happy. So then the greatest gods stopped to listen carefully, trying to figure out what the noise they were hearing meant, but they couldn't make sense of anything, because the noise was just that—noise.

"And since they couldn't dance to noise, the first gods, those who gave birth to the world, weren't able to walk, because for them walking was dancing. So they stood still and were very sad when they stopped walking, because they were great walkers, those first and greatest gods.

"Some of the gods tried to walk, or rather dance, to the noise, but it was impossible. They lost the beat, and they

17

lost their way, and they bumped into each other and fell and tripped on trees and stones and really hurt themselves." Old Antonio stops to relight the cigarette that the rain and noise had put out. After the flame comes the smoke; after the smoke follows the word: "So then the gods went out looking for silence to get their bearings again, but they couldn't find it anywhere. No one knew where it had gone—and understandably so, since there was so much noise. The greatest gods became desperate, because they didn't have the silence they needed to find their way. So they came to an agreement in an assembly of the gods, and they struggled a lot to make the assembly work, because there was so much noise. Finally, they agreed that each god would search for silence to find a path, and they were happy with their agreement, although you wouldn't have known it, because there was so much noise. Then each of the gods started to search for silence in order to find their way. They searched left and right... and found nothing. They searched high... nothing. They searched low... nothing. Since there was nowhere else to look, they had to search inside themselves. They looked within and searched for silence there. It was there that the greatest gods, those first ones who gave birth to the world, found silence and found themselves and, once again, found their way."

Old Antonio fell silent, and so did the rain. The silence didn't last long; quickly the crickets came, shattering the last remnants of that February night ten years ago.

Dawn was already breaking on the horizon when Old Antonio said goodbye, with "Well, I've arrived." *I stayed, inhaling the few bits of silence that the dawn had forgotten in the noisy mountains of the Mexican Southeast.*

The Story of the Others
January 20, 1998

It is dawn once again. Under a menacing airplane, la Mar tries to read a book of poetry in the faint glow of a dwindling candle.* I scribble away at a letter to someone I don't know in person, who perhaps speaks a different language, has another culture, probably is from another country, may be of a different color, and without a doubt has a different history. The plane goes by, and I stop, partly to listen, but mostly to give myself time to resolve the problem of how to write a letter to those who are different. Just at that moment, unseen by la Mar, Old Antonio appears next to me out of the high mountain fog. Tapping me on the back, he lights his cigarette and tells...

"The Story of the Others"

"The eldest of the elders who first inhabited these lands tell us that the greatest gods, the ones who gave birth to the world, did not all think alike. That is, they didn't have the same thoughts. They each had their own thoughts, yet they respected and listened to one another.

"The eldest of the elders say, of course, that's how it was. If it hadn't been that way, the world would never have been born,

---

* La Mar refers not to the sea (*el mar*) but to a woman, Marcos' romantic partner, whom he calls La Mar.

since those first gods would have spent all their time squabbling, because they each had different thoughts.

"The eldest of the elders say that this is why the world turned out with so many colors and shapes—as many as the thoughts that the greatest gods had, the very first ones. Seven were the greatest gods, and seven were the thoughts that each one had, and seven times seven are the shapes and colors with which they dressed the world."

Old Antonio tells me that he asked the eldest of the elders how those first gods ever agreed on anything or talked to one another if the thoughts they each had were so different. The eldest of the elders, Old Antonio tells me, explained to him that there had been an assembly of the seven gods and the seven different thoughts that each brought, and that in that assembly they reached an agreement.

Old Antonio says that the eldest of the elders told him that the assembly of the first gods, those who gave birth to the world, happened very long ago, so long ago, in fact, that time didn't exist yet. And the elders said that in that assembly each of the gods spoke their word, and each said, "The thoughts I have are different from those of the others." At that point, the gods fell silent, because they realized that when each of them said "the others" they meant different "others."

After they had been silent for a while, the first gods realized that they now had their first agreement: there were "others," and those "others" were different from themselves. In this way, the first agreement reached by the very first gods was to recognize difference and accept the existence of the other. But, then, what choice did they have since they were, after all, gods, first gods, and so they had to accept one another, not as greater or lesser but as different. They just had to keep on walking like that.

The discussion continued after that first agreement, because it is one thing to recognize that there are others who are different and something else entirely to respect them. So they spent a long while talking and discussing how each of them was different from the others. They didn't care that they were spending so much time talking, because, as it happens, time didn't exist yet. Then they all fell silent as each one spoke of their own difference. Each of the other gods realized that the more they listened and recognized the difference of the others, the more they discovered what it was within themselves that made them different. That made them very happy, and they started to dance. They danced for a long time, but that didn't bother them, because time didn't exist yet—not at that time.

"After all their dancing, they came to an agreement: it is good that there are others who are different, and it is necessary to listen to them to know ourselves. After they had reached this agreement, they went to sleep, because they were very tired from so much dancing. Talking didn't tire them out, because the first gods, the ones who gave birth to the world, had no problem talking—but listening, that's another thing. They were barely beginning to learn how to listen."

I didn't notice when Old Antonio left. La Mar is already sleeping and, of the candle, all that remains is a shapeless spot of wax. Above, the blackness of the night sky begins to dissolve in the glow of the future.

The Story of the Lion
and the Mirror
July 17, 1998

Old Antonio tells how when he was young his father Don Antonio taught him how to kill a lion without a firearm. Old Antonio says that when he was young Antonio, and his father was the old Antonio, his father told him the story that he now whispers in my ear so that La Mar can hear it from my lips. Old Antonio gets right to the story, but I've given it a name.

"The Story of the Lion and the Mirror"

"First, the lion dismembers his victim, then he drinks its blood, eats the heart, and leaves what remains for the vultures. There is nothing that can overpower the strength of the lion. There exists no animal that can stand up to him or any person who does not flee from him. Only a force as brutal, bloody, and powerful as the lion can defeat the lion."

Around the campfire, then old Antonio, father of then young Antonio rolled his cornhusk cigarette. Pretending to fix his attention on the burning logs that converged into a luminous star of fire, he looked at young Antonio out of the corner of his eye. He didn't wait long before young Antonio asked: "So what is this force strong enough to defeat the lion?"

Then old Antonio extended a mirror toward then young Antonio.

"Me?" *asked then young Antonio, looking at himself in the little round mirror.*

Then old Antonio smiled good-naturedly—at least that's what the man who was then young Antonio tells me now—and took the mirror back.

"No, not you," *he answered.*

"By showing you the mirror, I meant to say that the force able to kill the lion was that of the lion itself. Only the lion can defeat the lion."

"Ah!" *then young Antonio tells me he said, just to say something.*

Then old Antonio understood that then young Antonio had not understood anything and continued the story: "When we finally understood that only the lion could defeat the lion, we began to think about how to make the lion come face to face with himself. The eldest of the elders in the community said that it was necessary to get to know the lion, so they chose a young man for the task."

"You?" *interrupted then young Antonio.*

Then old Antonio did not disagree. Silently, he shifted the logs of the campfire and continued: "They raised the young man to the top of a ceiba tree, and at the foot of the tree they tied up a calf. Then they left. The young man was to observe what the lion did to the calf, wait until the lion left, and return to the community to tell what he had seen. So it happened: the lion arrived and killed and dismembered the calf. Then he drank its blood, ate its heart, and left as the vultures circled overhead, awaiting their turn.

"The young man went back to his community and told what he had seen. The eldest of the elders thought for a while and then said, 'Let the killer die the same way he kills.' They gave the young man a mirror, some horseshoe nails, and a calf.

"'Tomorrow will be the night of justice,' said the elders and returned to their thoughts. The young man didn't understand. He returned home and stayed there for quite a while contemplating the puzzle before him. That's how his father found him when he arrived and asked what was going on. The young man told him everything. His father remained silent by his side. After a while, he spoke. Listening to his father, the young man began to smile.

"The following day, when the afternoon was turning gold and the grey of night was descending over the tops of the trees, the young man left the community and went to the foot of the ceiba tree with the calf. When he arrived at the foot of the mother tree, he killed the calf and wrenched out its heart. He then broke the mirror into many little pieces and stuck them to the heart with the calf's own blood. Next, he tore open the heart and filled it with the horseshoe nails. He returned the heart to the calf's chest, and with stakes fashioned a frame to keep the calf standing as if it were alive. The young man climbed to the top of the ceiba and waited. Up there, as night descended from the trees to the ground, he recalled the words of his father: 'The same death with which the killer kills will be his own death.'

"All was night in the time below when the lion finally arrived. The animal approached and with one leap attacked the calf and dismembered it. When he licked the heart, the lion became suspicious because the blood was dry. But by then the broken pieces of the mirror had wounded the lion's tongue, making it bleed. That's how the lion came to think that his own blood was blood from the calf's heart. Intoxicated, he sunk his teeth deep into the heart. The horseshoe nails made him bleed even more, but the lion continued to think that the blood in his mouth was the calf's. The more the lion chewed, the more he wounded himself, and the more he bled, the more he chewed.

"The lion continued like that until he bled to death.

"The young man returned home wearing the lion's claws as a necklace and showed it to the eldest of the elders in the community. They smiled and said to him, 'It isn't the claws that you should keep as a victory trophy but the mirror.'"

"That," *Old Antonio says,* "is how to kill a lion." *But in addition to a mirror, Old Antonio always carries with him his flintlock shotgun.* "Just in case the lion doesn't know the story." *Old Antonio smiles and winks.*

Forever and Never
against Sometimes
September 12, 1998

Once upon a time, there were two times. One was called *One Time* and the other was called *Another Time*. *One Time* and *Another Time* together made the *Sometimes* family, who lived and ate from time to time. The great dominant empires were *Forever* and *Never*, which, as you would imagine, loathed the *Sometimes* family. *Forever* and *Never* couldn't stand the very existence of the *Sometimes* family. *Forever* could not allow *One Time* to live in its kingdom, because it would stop being *Forever*, since the existence of one time means there is no forever. Similarly, *Never* could not allow *Another Time* to appear another time in its kingdom, because *Never* cannot live with one time, much less so if that time is another time. But *One Time* and *Another Time* continued to bother *Forever* and *Never* time and time again. So it was, until *Forever* left them in peace forever and *Never* did not bother them ever again. After that, *One Time* and *Another Time* passed their time playing, all the time.

"What is it this time?" *One Time* would ask, and *Another Time* would reply, "Can't you see?" So, as you can see, they lived happily—from time to time and forever remained *One Time* and *Another Time* and never stopped being *Sometimes*.

Tan tan.

Moral 1: Sometimes it is very hard to distinguish between one time and another time.

Moral 2: You must never say forever (well, sometimes it's okay).
Moral 3: The *Forevers* and *Nevers* are imposed from above, but below there appear, time and time again, "the troublemakers," which sometimes is another name for "those who are different" or, at times, "rebels."
Moral No. 4: Never ever again will I write a story like this one, and I always do what I say (well, okay, sometimes I don't).

Vale y salud, and sometimes *Forever* and *Never* come from below (below the belly, for instance).

The Story of Looking
August 11, 1999

A spiral of smoke slowly leaves Old Antonio's mouth. Contemplating it, he begins to shape it into sign and word. After the smoke and the rumination come his words...

"Look, Captain." (*I should clarify that at the time I met Old Antonio, I held the title of Second Captain of Rebel Infantry, which was nothing more than typical Zapatista sarcasm, since at that time there were only four of us—that's why Old Antonio calls me "Captain."*) "Look, Captain, there was a time, a long time ago, when no one looked.

"It isn't that the men and women who walked these lands didn't have eyes; of course, they did, but they didn't look. The greatest gods, those who gave birth to the world, the very first ones, had indeed given birth to many things, but without making clear why they were created or for what purpose, that is to say, what was their reason for being? Or what was the work that each thing was to do or try to do? Did each thing have a reason for being? Well, yes, because the gods who gave birth to the world, the very first ones, were, of course, the greatest, and they knew quite well the why and wherefore of each thing. They were gods, after all.

"But it turns out that these first gods didn't worry so much about what they were doing. They did everything as if it were a party, a game, a dance. In fact, the eldest of the elders say that when the first gods got together, you could bet there would be a marimba around, because there was always singing and dancing after an assembly. Not only that; they say that if there was no marimba, there simply wouldn't be any assembly, and the gods would just sit there, scratching their bellies, telling jokes, and pulling pranks.

"Anyway, the thing is, the greatest gods, the first ones, gave birth to the world, yes, but they didn't clearly explain the why or wherefore of each thing, of eyes, for example.

"You would think the gods might have mentioned that eyes were for looking, but, no. That is why the first men and women who walked the earth went about stumbling and hurting themselves, falling and bumping into one another, grabbing things they didn't want and missing the things they did, just as many people do today: taking things they don't want, which cause them harm; failing to take the things they need, which would make them better; tripping and bumping into one another.

"All this is to say that the first men and women did indeed have eyes. They had them, but they didn't look. Their eyes came in countless varieties: all kinds of colors and shapes and sizes. There were round eyes, almond eyes, oval eyes, tiny eyes, big eyes, medium eyes, black eyes, blue eyes, yellow eyes, green eyes, brown eyes, red eyes, and white eyes. Many eyes, yes, two of them for each of the first men and women, but still they didn't see anything.

"It would have continued like that until today, if it weren't for the fact that one day something happened. The thing is that the first gods, those who gave birth to the world, the great ones, were dancing because it was August, the month of memories and tomorrows,* when suddenly some of the men and women

---

* August as the month of memories and tomorrows likely refers to August 6, 1969, the date of the founding of the Fuerzas de Liberación Nacional, in Monterrey, by the brothers Fernando, César, and Pedro Yáñez. For a discussion, see the commentary to the story "We Who Came After Did Understand." August 2003, when the caracoles were officially founded, is one of those tomorrows.

who didn't look wandered into the place where the gods were having their party and crashed right into them, while others ran into the marimba and knocked it over. The party turned into a total mess; the music and singing stopped, and so did the dancing. It was chaos. The first gods were running all over the place trying to figure out why the party had stopped, while the men and women who didn't look just kept on tripping and bumping into the gods and into one another. They continued like that for quite a while, falling and crashing and swearing and cursing one another.

"Finally, the greatest gods figured out that the whole upheaval had begun with the arrival of those first men and women. So the gods gathered them together to give them a talking to and asked them if they even bothered to look where they were going. These first men and women didn't look at each other, because, well, they didn't look. Instead, they asked what does *to look* mean? And then the gods who gave birth to the world realized that they hadn't made clear what eyes were for, or, rather, what their reason for being was: the wherefore and why of eyes. So the greatest gods explained to the first men and women what 'looking' was and taught them to look. That's how men and women learned that you can look at others, know that they exist, they are there, they are other, and, in that way, not bump into them, hurt, step over, or trip them.

"They also learned that they could look inside another and see what their hearts are feeling, since the heart doesn't always speak with words that come from the lips. Many times, the heart speaks with the skin, with a look, or by walking.

"They also learned to look at those who see only themselves, who see only themselves in others' looks.

"And they learned to look at those others who look at them looking.

"The first men and women learned every type of gaze there was, and the most important one they learned is the gaze that looks at itself and is aware of itself and knows itself, that sees itself both looking and looking inward, that sees paths and futures yet to be born, paths not yet walked, and dawns yet to break.

"Once these men and women learned this, the gods who gave birth to the world charged them—the very same ones who had arrived tripping and bumping and falling on their faces— with the task of teaching other men and women how to look and what looking was for. That is how those who are different learned to look and look at themselves.

"But not everyone learned, because the world was already set in motion, and men and women were already moving about in every direction, tripping, falling, and bumping into one another. But some did learn, and those men and women who did learn to look are the ones known as the men and women of corn, the true people."

Old Antonio remained silent. I looked at him looking at me looking at him and turned away, fixing my gaze on some distant spot in the dawn sky.

Old Antonio looked where I was looking, and, without saying a word, waved the lit butt of his cornhusk cigarette. Suddenly, summoned by the light in his hand, a firefly emerged from the darkest corner of the night and tracing brief luminous swirls approached the spot where we were sitting. Old Antonio took the firefly between his fingers and, blowing gently bid it farewell. Away went the firefly, with its stuttering light.

For a while the night below remained dark. Suddenly, hundreds of fireflies began a brilliant chaotic dance, and the night below filled with as many stars as clothed that August night above in the mountains of the Mexican Southeast.

"To look and to struggle, it is not enough to know where to direct your gaze, patience, and effort," Old Antonio said to me as he got up. "One must also get started, reach out, and meet other gazes, which, in turn, will get started, reach out, and meet yet other gazes. In this way, looking at the other looking, many gazes are born, and the world sees that it can be better, and that there is room for all gazes and for those who, though different and other, look at others looking and see themselves walking a history yet to be made."

Old Antonio left. I stayed there through the dawn. When I relit my pipe, a thousand lights below made eyes light up, and there was light below, where there should be light and many different gazes...

Sisters and brothers, teachers and students, we hope that this meeting will be successful and will allow you to know and understand our way of looking.

We know that your gaze will know how to see us seeing you, and that your gaze will summon others, many others, and there will be a path and light so that, one day, people will no longer stumble at dawn.

Vale. *Salud, and to see far away you don't need binoculars, but the long view that dignity bestows on those who struggle and live it.*

We Who Came After
Did Understand
August 31, 1999

The story goes that there was once a town where the men and women worked very hard to live. Every day these men and women would leave for their respective tasks: the men to the fields of corn and beans, the women to haul firewood and carry water. However, some tasks brought them together without distinction. For example, when it was time to pick the coffee, both men and women joined together for the harvest. That's the way it was.

But there was one man who did none of that. He did work, of course, but not in the fields of corn and beans, nor did he show up to pick coffee when the berries turned red on their branches. None of that: this man worked planting trees on the mountain.

The trees that the man planted were not the fast-growing kind. It would take them entire decades to acquire their branches and leaves. The other men would laugh and criticize him. "Why do you work on things that you will never see finished? You should tend the milpa that bears fruit in just a few months, instead of planting trees that won't be fully grown until after you're already dead.

"You must be foolish or crazy, because your work is useless."

The man defended himself saying, "It's true I am not going to see these trees fully grown, with their branches, leaves, and birds, and my eyes won't see the children playing in their shade, but if we all work only for the present or, at most, for the next morning, who will plant the trees that our descendants will need for shelter, comfort, and happiness?"

No one understood him. The man, crazy or foolish, continued planting trees that he would never see, and the sensible men and women continued planting and working for their present.

Time took its toll, and they all passed away. Their children followed them in the same work, as did the children of their children. One morning, a group of boys and girls went for a walk and found a place full of giant trees. A thousand birds had made their home there. The vast canopy provided relief from the heat and protection from the rain. Yes, they had come upon an entire mountainside full of trees. The boys and girls returned to the town and told of this wondrous place.

The men and women gathered there and were astonished.

"Who planted these trees?" they asked one another.

No one knew. They went to talk with their elders, who didn't know either. Only one old man, the oldest in the community, was able to give them an explanation, and he told them the story of the crazy and foolish man.

The men and women called an assembly and talked amongst themselves. They then saw and understood the man their ancestors had known, and they greatly admired and loved that man.

Because they knew that memory can travel very far and arrive where no one thinks or imagines, the men and women of the present went to the place of the great trees.

They surrounded a tree that stood in the center. There, they made a sign with colorful letters. Afterwards, they threw a party. The dawn was already upon them when the last dancers went to sleep.

The forest was left silent and alone. It rained, and then stopped raining. The Moon came out, and the Milky Way once again unwound its twisted body. Suddenly, a beam of moonlight managed to slip through the great branches and leaves of the tree at the center and, with its dim light, was able to read the colorful sign that was left there. It said: "To the first ones: we who came after did understand. *Salud.*"

The Story of the Night Air
March 8, 2000

Old Antonio had let the morning and afternoon pass with the same calm with which he now lit his cigarette. For an instant, a bat darted around us, most likely disturbed by the light Old Antonio was using to give life to the tobacco. Just like the bat, the tzotz, *there also appeared, suddenly, in the middle of the night…*

"The Story of the Night Air"

When the greatest gods, those who gave birth to the world, the very first ones, thought about how and why they were going to do what they were going to do, they held an assembly, where each one brought forth their word in order to know it and so that the others could know it. In this way, each one of the very first gods would draw out a word and throw it into the center of the assembly, and there it would bounce and arrive at another god, who would pick it up and toss it again, and so, like a ball, the word would pass from one side to the other until everyone understood it, and then they would make their agreement, those greatest gods, the ones who gave birth to all the things that we call worlds. One of the agreements they came to when they brought forth their words was that each path would have its walker, and each walker a path. So things were born complete, each with its other.

That is how the air and the birds were born. That is, there was not first air and later birds to move in it, nor were birds made first and later air so they could fly. It was the same with water and the fish that swim in it, earth and the animals that walk on it, the path and the feet that travel it. Speaking of birds—there was one bird that protested bitterly against the air.

This bird said that he would be able to fly better and faster if it weren't for the air's resistance. He would complain, because even though his flight was quick and agile he always wanted it to be faster and better, and, if it wasn't, that was because, according to him, the air was an obstacle. The gods became irritated with this bird who flew in the air, yet did nothing but complain about it. So as punishment, the first gods took away his feathers and the light from his eyes. Naked, they sent him into the cold of the night. Blind, he was made to fly. Once graceful and swift, his flight became erratic and clumsy.

But when he regained his bearings, after countless stumbles and collisions, the bird figured out a way to see with his ears. By speaking to things, this bird, the tzotz (bat), orients himself and comes to know the world, which responds to him in language that only he knows how to hear. Without feathers to cover him, blind, and with a nervous and ungainly flight, the bat reigns over the night in the mountains. There is no animal that walks better than he does through the dark night air.

It was from this bird, the tzotz, the bat, that the true men and women learned to recognize the greatness and power of the spoken word, the sound of thought. They also learned that the night conceals many worlds, and that one must know how to listen for them in order to draw them out and allow them to flower. The worlds that the night contains are born with words. As they are uttered, they become lights, and they are so numerous that they do not fit on the earth, and many end up finding a place in the sky. This is why they say that stars are born on the ground.

The greatest gods also gave birth to men and women, not so that one would be the path of the other but so that each would be at once both path and walker. They were made different so that they could be together. The greatest gods made men and women so that they could love each other. That is why the night air is so good for taking flight, for thinking, for talking, and for making love.

The Commentaries

Antonio's Dream and a Prophecy

This fragment is the conclusion of a notable piece titled "Chiapas: The Southeast in Two Winds, a Storm and a Prophecy." Published on January 27, 1994, it was originally written by Subcomandante Insurgente Marcos two years earlier, in August 1992.[1] At that time, while the Zapatistas were still secretly organizing their movement, the purpose of the piece was to "awaken the consciousness" of compañeros who had joined their ranks or had shown interest in their struggle. A year and a half later, given the curiosity and the emotions stirred across Mexico by the January 1, 1994, uprising in Chiapas, the Zapatistas made this document public with a similar purpose: to satisfy the country's need for information about the conditions that motivated the revolt in "the mountains of the Mexican Southeast."

As we read the complete text with a mixture of delight at the style and fury at the facts, we are reminded of other remarkable denunciations of colonial exploitation, such as Eduardo Galeano's *Open Veins of Latin America* (1971) and Jonathan Swift's *A Modest Proposal for Preventing the Children of Poor People in Ireland from Being a Burthen to Their Parents or Country, and for Making Them Beneficial to the Publick* (1729). "The Southeast in Two Winds" is a parody of a modern tourist guide to Chiapas that, instead of attractions, lists a barrage of hard social facts and economic statistics, illustrating the dire life conditions for Chiapas's majority Indian population.

That parody in turn is framed within a satiric imitation of an early modern novel about an evil viceroy (Carlos Salinas de Gortari, president of Mexico from 1988 to 1894) and his long-suffering subjects. Just as the viceroy of yesterday served Spain, today's Mexican government serves the distant empire to the North, which, at the time of the Zapatista uprising, has proclaimed the death of socialism after the fall of the Soviet Union. In the heart of the Indigenous mountains, however, that message, welcomed by the powerful viceroy and his friends, is not embraced by those others who perceive a different wind, "from below and to the left." The sweeping wind of neoliberal globalization above and the communities' uncompromising resistance to it below: this is the confrontation that has continued to shape the Zapatista struggle until today. As the viceroy worries and has fearful nightmares about the winds of discontent, Antonio and those below dream that they are many and that a better world is possible. We now know that soon after this dream, or prophecy, they will all wake up from the nightmare of history to the Zapatista cry of "¡Ya basta!"

At the very end of this long communiqué, as our fragment begins, a young character suddenly makes his entrance: Antonio. Husband, father, peasant—and dreamer. He is both a literary character and, as Marcos tells us in a communiqué issued on May 28, 1994, an actual person. In real life, he is the son of that "Old Antonio" Marcos had met ten years before the uprising, who became his guide into the local culture and history of political organizing. "A sort of translator," "a bridge" between the urban guerrillas and the Indigenous communities in the Lacandon Jungle, "Old Antonio" is the narrator of many of the creation stories or fables that Marcos tells, including those in this collection. Like his son, he is both a character and a living person—just as the Zapatistas are both icons of resistance and real people.

In the May 28 communiqué, Marcos talks about both Antonios in two scenes that, read together with the above prophecy, constitute three foundational elements of Zapatista poetics and history: the prophecy, the communal assembly, and rebellion—the imagination of the future, the internal democratic process, the refusal to give up.

In the first scene, Marcos reminisces about having been with Old Antonio and young Antonio in 1992. He was visiting the towns in the Lacandon Jungle to gather the communities' responses regarding a life-and-death decision: whether or not to declare war on the Mexican government. When he reached the community of the Antonios, young Antonio was charged with delivering the message to the townspeople, who, gathered in their assembly in the village school, were to decide whether or not to go to war: a significant, if not the most significant, moment in Zapatista history.

As Marcos and Old Antonio waited outside, Old Antonio guided Marcos to the banks of the quiet river below the town. Here begins the second scene. Sitting there, Old Antonio pointed out the contrast between the calm, clear waters at their feet and the alarming view at the top of the nearest mountain, with its menacing clouds and bolts of lightning shattering the diffuse blue of the mountain top. There was a true storm happening above, where the streams gather strength to begin their powerful descent. Once that happens, Old Antonio explained, once they start rushing down, the peaceful river by which they now sit will roar, overflow its banks with violent waters, and renew the soil. Destruction will bring rebirth, as the river rebuilds the soil and helps transform it into corn, beans, and sugar to feed those who live there. Force is born in the mountains, but you don't see it until it comes down, concludes Old Antonio, and then he clarifies the meaning of this to Marcos: you, the EZLN, are the streams. It is time for the streams to come down.

Silently, as night was falling, the two walked back up to the town, where young Antonio handed them the agreement that had been reached by the people, which according to Marcos read roughly: "The men, women, and children assembled at the school in the community to see in their hearts if it was time to begin the war for freedom. They split into three groups to debate: women, children, and men. After that, we all came back together in the schoolhouse and the majority reached the conclusion that the war had to begin, because Mexico was already selling itself off to foreigners, and while hunger may come and go, if we are no longer Mexicans, that will be forever. This agreement was reached by twelve men, twenty-three women, and eight children capable of reasoning and was signed by all those who knew how; those who didn't, signed with their thumbprint."

Such assemblies were described equally memorably by Bishop Samuel Ruiz, who was himself transformed by *la palabra quemante* (the burning word) of the Indians. Their blunt and pained descriptions of the harsh conditions of their lives, in fact, led him to change the Church's method of teaching. Instead of *reflexión prefabricada* (indoctrination by rote), the catechists would now proceed by gathering the community's own thinking. This is how he recorded the results: "Reflecting on very painful lived situations, men, and women and children as well, intervened, discussing all at the same time and in loud voices, as is the Indigenous way, until the 'accord' arose that contained their vision."[2]

Around March 1994, Old Antonio died of tuberculosis. But his stories and his memory lived on, guiding Marcos through the years each time he found himself facing an impossible situation. While it is through Marcos's writing that we know Old Antonio, the great storyteller, we do not know to what extent he and his fables are a product of Marcos's imagination, but we do know that, in addition to mythic stories, he transmitted the cultural and political memories of a long and intense life. Through the careful research of historian Jan de Vos, we learn that Old Antonio was the bearer of historical memory among his people, as well as for a newcomer like Marcos. Indeed, as a child he had lived with his parents, who were *peones acasillados* (debt peons) tied to a Chiapas hacienda regime of exploitation. In the 1930s, when the agrarian reform of President Lázaro Cárdenas brought the promise of the Mexican Revolution to Chiapas, Old Antonio obtained land. He participated with his children and other relatives during the 1960s and 1970s mobilization of campesinos in Northern Chiapas. He also participated in the founding of two new ejidos in the Lacandon Jungle,[3] Emiliano Zapata and Tierra y Libertad, now autonomous Zapatista communities. It is also possible that, in addition to his son, young Antonio, he was the father of Major Ana María of the EZLN.[4] His life, thus, seems to encompass the history of a whole region and many of its people, in motion through the twentieth century, determined in their search for land and a dignified future. Since the Lacandon Jungle was settled mostly by young people, they may have learned from him and others like him the past of their communities on their long road to the future.[5]

Durito and Zapata Do Remember

The day on which Durito's story appeared, April 10, 1994, was the anniversary of two significant historical events in Mexico: the seventy-fifth anniversary of the assassination of Emiliano Zapata, the revolutionary peasant leader of the Army of the South, and the hundredth day since the EZLN's uprising against the bad government. The Zapatistas named themselves after Emiliano Zapata and his followers to signal their identification with and admiration for those earlier rebels, who, like them, fought for land restitution and justice for Indigenous communities.

The land guarantees won by the Mexican Revolution were upended by the government of Carlos Salinas de Gortari, Mexico's president from 1988 to 1994. While falsely claiming the legacy of Zapata for himself, Salinas actually dismantled it by revising Article 27 of the Mexican constitution, bringing an end to land redistribution and to communal land tenure, the ejido.[1]

Ejido lands became private property that could be bought and sold. These constitutional changes carried out in 1992 were a precondition set by the US for Mexico to enter into the North American Free Trade Agreement (NAFTA) in 1994. Once established, the new regime of private property in land would not only open the way to foreign investment; it would erase the memory of any other mode of living and being.[2] It was a decisive step toward the legalization of a neoliberal economic regime in which traditional values metamorphose into commodities. And this is what profoundly worries both Durito and Marcos and makes more significant the date of the publication: the achievements of Emiliano Zapata seem to be crumbling, his assassination looms as tragic as in the distant past, but the two friends reassure each other that this time things will be alright.

In our story, Marcos introduces us to a new character, Durito, a pipe-smoking beetle who worries about being crushed under soldiers' boots as he ponders war and neoliberalism's designs on Latin America. Like a well-trained Marxist—presumably, the Sup's alter ego—Durito studies all the factors surrounding the Zapatista uprising: "the objective conditions, the maturity of the subjective conditions, the correlation of forces, the crisis of imperialism, the crisis of socialism, etc., etc." After much elaborate deliberation, Durito concludes that the Zapatistas will win the war, but that it will take a long time—a conclusion that, though heartening, Marcos finds unilluminating. In terms of the immediate future, however, they share the concern of being crushed, in Marcos's case not by boots (or not primarily by boots) but by what he will call elsewhere "The Fourth World War" unleashed by neoliberal economics.[3]

Although this story was presented to the public on April 10, 1994, it recounts the first meeting of Marcos and Durito a decade earlier. On December 25, 1985, Durito came during the "asphyxiating solitude of the first years of the Zapatista guerrilla." They met again in March 1995, and he continued to appear in many stories after that, whether as a detective, a political analyst, a knight-errant, a one-eyed pirate, a bull-fighter, or a writer of letters.[4] He is the narrator of one of our stories, "The Story of the Little Cat and the Little Mouse," and in subsequent communiqués he will help Marcos refine his analysis of neoliberalism and provide commentary on whatever, often desperate, political situation confronts the Zapatistas.

If, in this story, he appears as messenger from the other beetles concerned about being crushed under the boots of soldiers of the Mexican army and the EZLN, he continues to show up in different situations and varied personas, adding a distinctively Zapatista humor to the serious business of critical thinking in the complex political terrain in which the EZLN must maneuver. With protean adaptability, in 2020, Durito becomes Melville's Ishmael; while in our story above he is the biblical character or possibly Rubén Darío's Nebuchadnezzar;[5] in several others, he is Don Quijote de la Mancha or Don Durito de la Lacandona.

On Moles, Lions, and Democracy

"The Lion Kills by Looking" was published three days after the presidential election of August 21, 1994, when the results had awarded victory, as usual, to the PRI (Partido Revolucionario Institucional)[1]—the nemesis of the Zapatistas. Of more immediate concern, the PRI candidate for governor of Chiapas was imposed by fraud against Amado Avendaño, the founder and editor of the newspaper *El Tiempo*, whom the Zapatistas had nominated and supported, and who would, from then on, govern "in rebellion."

The story is organized around two motifs that had previously appeared in Zapatista writing: the figures of the heart and the mole. It retells an old story narrated to Marcos by Old Antonio, whose lesson now, nine years later, will hold the Zapatistas in good stead, even if the PRI remains in power: you must know "where to look," had counseled Old Antonio, so as to kill fear and not give up.

The story contrasts those who surrender to the terrifying stare of the lion (the state and its dominant forces) to those others—like the moles—who look inward to their heart and are, thus, immunized from the paralyzing consequences produced by the lion's gaze. Indeed, months earlier, the CCRI-CG had explicated this gesture of turning toward the heart,[2] not in the philosophical sense of "know thyself" or in the contemplative sense of religion but in the anthropological sense of culture as center. This happened in two messages dated March 1, 1994. In the first one, the CCRI states that they need to return home to discuss with their communities the government's counter-proposals to the Zapatistas' demands. Should they sign the peace accords? Had they obtained satisfaction of their main demands? Could they trust the government? It is to reach such a critical decision that they are returning to their communities, where they speak in the same tongue and have a shared sense of time. They say they are going back to their true heart to ask the heart what they should do next.

In the second communiqué, the CCRI writes in similar fashion that in order to reflect on the Peace Commissioner's words, they must "speak to the collective heart that commands us.... From them, from our own, from the Indigenous in the mountains and the jungle, will come the signal indicating the next step we must take on this road, whose destination will either be peace with justice and dignity, or else will not be."[3] The "collective heart," which here engages and takes shape in the discussions of the communal assemblies, will continue to guide the CCRI and the communities as they follow the principles of *mandar obedeciendo* (leading by obeying) and of advancing by *caminar preguntando* (asking questions and listening to others' thoughts).

The mole in its figurative sense is the second poetic motif, introduced in an initial distraught response to the assassination of the PRI's presidential candidate Luis Donaldo Colosio, shot in the head in public on camera. On March 24, as he bemoans the enormity of the event, Marcos addresses those he elsewhere calls the "faceless" ones in the mountains of the Mexican Southeast as "Zapatista brother moles (*topos*)," or even "beloved moles." Perhaps it will now be up to those *amados topos*—that is, the Zapatista bases of support—to continue the public work of the revolution—should the shocking murder of someone from the highest echelons of the political class serve as a harbinger of definitive state violence against the EZLN.[4]

Because it is handled here with such easy familiarity, it is likely that the figural use of the term "moles" was not introduced for the first time on March 24 but, on the contrary, was already known by Marcos's audience. For some of us, the term is not surprising either, since this image, which conveys the secrecy and *underground* work done by revolutionaries in the Selva Lacandona, segues into the symbolic use of the mole in Western Marxism. The image of the mole illustrates the hybridity of Marcos's poetics: it is both local and global. Local: we recall, for example, how many communities in the Lacandon Jungle supported and organized the uprising in total secrecy.[5] Like moles, they built their covert corridors in the dark side of history until they emerged, unexpectedly, on January 1, 1994. Global: borrowing the phrase from Shakespeare's *Hamlet*, Marx thought of revolution itself as an *old mole* that tunnels through the underground, creating invisible galleries of resistance until, gathering strength, suddenly, somewhere, revolution surfaces onto the illuminated stage of history with the force of an event. Chiapas, January 1, 1994, was such an event; since then, it has spread, in rhizomatic fashion to emerge in the vast world of global capitalism in faraway places, such as Seattle in 1999, Genoa and the World Social Forum in 2001, or, later, in the numerous adherents to the "Sexta" (Sixth Declaration of the Lacandon Jungle) since 2006 and Zapatista solidarity groups the world over, as evidenced during their trip to Europe in 2021.

As it turned out, after consultations with their communities and after the never satisfactorily explained assassination of Colosio, the Zapatistas rejected the narrow government offers. Abandoning a useless dialogue, they turned toward civil society and invited Mexicans of all walks of life with affinities to the main Zapatista positions to send representatives to a National Democratic Convention to meet in the jungle. They would discuss among themselves the future of the country. As unlikely as all this sounds, the event did take place in the Lacandon Jungle on August 6–9, 1994, in the town of Guadalupe Tepeyac, and it was attended by six thousand delegates from multiple organizations in Mexico.⁶ During the opening ceremony, Marcos handed over a Mexican flag to Rosario Ibarra, mother of a disappeared student and now president of the convention. At this point, the past connects with our story, no longer through the use of figural language, as in *heart* or *moles*, but through the materiality of the lion's skin: the flag of Mexico passed on to the convention's president had been wrapped for protection in that very same lion's skin that, as we read in "The Lion Kills by Looking," Old Antonio had once bequeathed to Marcos. The skin, preserved for so many years (since 1985), is an amulet of sorts, a reminder that *both the lion and fear are defeated by knowing where to look*. This was important advice at this point, after the national and local elections had been lost. "Do not surrender," the Sup has repeatedly exhorted sympathizers in Mexico and continued to do so after the electoral defeat: do not let the lion intimidate you with his mean stare. There is no word in Tzeltal, Tzotzil, or other Indigenous languages for the verb *surrender*, he had insisted in June. Now he framed this story by saying, "Do not sell out." And, yes, he says, trust your heart.

Coda

Women, Indigenous, Mexicans. Before Marcos handed the flag to Rosario Ibarra at the National Democratic Convention, the flag had passed through the hands of two Zapatista women. Major Ana María was in charge of the nearly a thousand troops who took over the Municipal Palace of the city of San Cristóbal de las Casas during the uprising. It was there that she announced, "We have recovered the flag," as she handed it to her commanders in the CCRI. During the ensuing peace negotiations, Comandanta Ramona carried the flag in her knapsack and eventually displayed it to the government representative as she declared: "We are Indians, and we are

Mexicans"—directly challenging the government's attempt to present the movement as secessionist. In "recovering" the Mexican flag from the government and later displaying it as also their own, the Zapatistas signaled a struggle over the vision of the country. That vision, here displayed by the diplomatic and military authority exercised by these two Indigenous women,[7] will become formalized in the Zapatista demand in the San Andrés negotiations for constitutional recognition of Indigenous peoples as subjects of law.

Not a Kids' Fable

This story is part of a letter written by Durito, who introduces himself in this appearance as a modern knight-errant. Like the hero Don Quixote, he is "the undoer of wrongs, restless dream of women, aspiration of men, the last and greatest exemplar of that race that ennobled humanity with colossal and selfless deeds, beetle, and moon warrior."[1] Readers will perhaps wonder if Marcos ever worries that Zapatista dreams could be as quixotic as the delusions of his alter ego.

Durito addresses his letter to delegates of Zapatista solidarity organizations from across Europe convening in Brescia, Italy, and more broadly to the peoples of the world. The activists had just participated in the Zapatistas' plebiscite to mobilize national and international solidarity with their demands to strengthen their hand in their negotiations with the government and determine their next steps. The Europeans tallied nearly three hundred thousand votes (1.3 million were registered in total, in Mexico and across the world), and at their meeting, they launched a Europe-wide Zapatista solidarity network. A year later, the Zapatistas would reciprocate by hosting a global conference: the First Intercontinental Encuentro for Humanity and against Neoliberalism.[2] The *Intergaláctico*, as it was called for short, held from July 27 to August 4, 1996, brought five thousand supporters from forty-two countries to Chiapas.

Because we first read this story as a children's fairy tale, its resolution can be startling; it leaves us wondering if it is a renewed justification of armed struggle—or an allusion to the Tom and Jerry cartoon. These incommensurable interpretations point to the fact that these tales, which appear simple, have a great power to disorient. In this one, the Zapatistas seem to be asking, or asking themselves, "What does a modern epic look like? Are we fighters in a grand struggle against neoliberalism—or cartoon characters?"

Indeed, throughout 1995, they had been engaged in a vicious game of cat and mouse with the Mexican government. Ernesto Zedillo (1994–2000) had assumed the presidency on December 1, 1994, with talk of dialogue and negotiations. Instead, in early February 1995, in the first of many betrayals by his government, he unleashed the Mexican army to pursue a scorched-earth policy, razing Zapatista homes and, in some cases, entire villages—in an effort to assassinate the members of the General Command and Subcomandante Marcos. Thousands were displaced, forced to flee to the mountains—in a rout that might have become a war of extermination had not massive demonstrations in Mexico and throughout the world demanded that the government call off their offensive. This national and international solidarity forced Zedillo back to a posture of negotiations. Unlike the little mouse, the Zapatistas did not resort to violence this time, but, like him, they began to realize that negotiating with the government might be a futile exercise.

The slapstick comedy serves as a way to present to those distant solidarity activists in Brescia the Zapatistas' current situation in a self-deprecating manner. They laugh at themselves, at their repeated and useless attempts to negotiate with the cat, at their misery and hunger, preparing their readers to share their desire to say ¡Ya Basta! once again, even as they keep negotiating. In the spirit of the cartoon, they let the story run away from them, concluding with the symbolic comic relief of feasting together on the roasted government.

Like the little mouse who grabs a machine gun and breaks out of the fable into history, in 1994, the Zapatistas shattered the celebratory consensus around NAFTA and neoliberal globalization when they rose up in arms. The government was forced to stop the war and negotiate, because Mexicans massively took to the streets to demand a cease-fire. At this point, in 1995, as the slow-moving negotiations continued, they sensed another fairy tale. Still wary of the government's intentions, they turned again to civil society and their international friends and held a plebiscite... to ask what their next steps should be! Surely an unexpected—perhaps unprecedented—move in the history of revolutions.

It is in those exits from predictable plots that history begins again.

About the Strategy and Shape of Struggle

"The Story of the Sword, the Tree, the Stone, and the Water" appeared in a communiqué titled "And After the Plebiscite. Now What?" Written by Marcos, it summarizes the results of that national and international plebiscite the Zapatistas had called in August to determine their next steps. More than 1.3 million people in Mexico and around the world organized to reply to the questions posed by an armed group cornered in the mountains in Southeast Mexican. Based on the results of the plebiscite, with national and international solidarity continuing to expand, the Zapatistas had enough support to continue the San Andrés negotiations with the Mexican Government.

A great part of this communiqué is an eloquent acknowledgement of the solidarity work of so many—Marcos singles out for recognition artists, young people, homosexuals, prisoners, and women—all of whom contributed to the success of the *consulta*: in Mexico, on the American continent, and across the world.

This new story by Old Antonio illustrates different modes of struggle through which the Indigenous have resisted for five hundred years. His story ends with him saying, "The strangers went away. We are still here. Like the water of the stream, we continue to walk toward the river that will carry us to the vast waters where the greatest gods, those who gave birth to the world, the first ones, quench their thirst." He proposes that, in this moment of crisis, the Zapatistas should flow, unperturbed, like calm water.

Since 1994, the EZLN and the Zapatista bases of support have continued to organize and strengthen their communities internally. But they recognize—and that is the point of the consulta—that only when their struggle has flowed into those of others, only when the Zapatista streams have enriched and been enriched by other lands and other rivers, in Mexico, and ultimately the world, only then will they reach the ocean, and, there, like the greatest gods, finally quench their thirst— for justice, peace, and dignity. This is the Zapatistas' utopian project, affirmed here again; their struggle is not only for the Indigenous, or for Mexico, but for the world.

Muting the Sound of War

This story is part of a letter addressed to the national and international press, in the face of the government's apparent return to the military option of two years earlier. While the government feigned negotiations with the Zapatistas, it repeatedly aborted them, terrorizing the population with sudden incursions of soldiers, planes, and tanks. The starkest example of this schizophrenia is the case of the San Andrés Accords. Signed in February 1996, they granted local political autonomy, collective control over natural resources, and cultural rights to the Indigenous inhabitants of Mexico—but they never became law. In early 1997, the Zapatistas denounced the federal government's failure to have ever negotiated in good faith, instead using the dialogues to buy time, always with the intention of finishing what they failed to do in 1995: to assassinate the leadership of the EZLN.

"The Story of Noise and Silence" opposes the pretense of negotiations that are just "so much noise" to the repeated tactical retreats into silence of the Zapatistas, or, as the story would have it, into their own hearts. It tells of the first gods, who, "in the time before time," walked by dancing, or didn't distinguish between the two. But the gods couldn't hear the rhythm, they lost their balance and stumbled, because instead of music there was only "a lot of noise and none of it made sense." Old Antonio told the story to Marcos in 1987 amid deafening jungle rains. At present, the Sup is describing different kinds of noise, ranging from military airplanes over Chiapas to electoral spectacles on TV and the incessant government monologue—both at home and abroad.

Indeed, in a communiqué issued a few days after our story, Marcos reports that the Mexican Secretary of Foreign Affairs, at that very moment in Europe trying to woo investors with reassurances of military and political control of the country, was met with uncomfortable questions about human rights violations from his European hosts, following widespread popular mobilizations in support of the Zapatistas.[1]

Marcos extends deep gratitude to those whose solidarity kept the military assault on the Zapatistas from succeeding or passing unnoticed, recognizing that those activists had taken the trouble to learn about the situation of the Zapatistas in Chiapas, in the face of media and government lies. He says that this bridge of solidarity invites a return crossing on the part of the Zapatistas, who are moved to learn about the struggles out of which such solidarity grew. Not until 2021 would this aspiration take shape—in the Zapatistas' listening tour to Europe, the first in their planned five-continent expedition. As we were completing these commentaries, their plan materialized, and we have followed their first group traveling by sailboat to Spain,[2] reversing the voyage of the Spanish who conquered Tenochtitlan in 1521. More seriously, the Zapatistas have explained that they intend to learn firsthand about the struggles of their European allies who have so forcefully supported them since the first years of the uprising.[3]

A World Connected through Solidarity

Marcos wrote "The Story of the Others" as part of a communiqué called "The Struggle for Peace and Humanity Is Intercontinental." The story explores some of the conundrums of solidarity. It is addressed to all the people in Mexico and twenty-seven other countries who took to the streets to denounce the brutal massacre that had occurred at Acteal on December 22, 1997. To fully understand Acteal's impact and the outrage it engendered, we recount here some of the specifics of that day.

On that date, a band of some one hundred paramilitaries murdered forty-five Tzotzil civilians who had taken refuge in a church in the town of Acteal, most of them women and children. The dead were members of Las Abejas (The Bees), a pacifist organization influenced by liberation theology and openly sympathetic to the EZLN. For the Zapatistas, these murders were "the worst crime in the last thirty years"—comparable to the notorious massacre of university students in Tlatelolco Plaza in 1968. The gruesome chasing down and shooting of victims that ensued that December day lasted for hours—with the army stationed nearby and local police and authorities refusing to intervene. This was neither an accident nor an isolated incident. Indeed, soon after the crime, it was revealed in the magazine *Proceso* that as early as 1994 the military had developed plans for a counterinsurgency war in

Chiapas, whose centerpiece was the use of Indigenous para-militaries to terrorize communities, displace populations, and erode support for the EZLN—precisely what was enacted most brutally at Acteal.[1]

Despite these revelations, at the end of January, con-fronted by the press at the World Economic Forum in Davos, President Zedillo (1994–2000) insisted that the government had nothing to do with Acteal. The international explosion of protest and thousands of letters demanding justice, including a resolution from the European Union,[2] unnerved the Mexican government, which proceeded to reject such denunciations as "*injerencia* (intervention) in its internal affairs. The Zapatistas, for their part, agreed with their supporters abroad that "the struggle for peace and humanity must be intercontinental." This is important: since the first weeks following the upris-ing, the Zapatistas have always fought for a better world—not only for a better Chiapas—and made (and continue to make) extraordinary efforts to connect with the world. The world below and to the left, of course—but the world.

In this communiqué, Marcos writes to assure support-ers around the world that their cries of solidarity and outrage had reached and moved the Zapatistas in Chiapas. But how, he asks, does one write a letter "to someone I don't know in person, who perhaps speaks a different language, has another culture, probably is from another country, may be of a differ-ent color, and without a doubt has a different history?" Marcos finds himself stumped by this question, until the ghost of Old Antonio appears with a story to help him. The story elaborates and apparently resolves Marcos's perplexity.

Old Antonio takes us to foundational times when the first seven gods had to reckon with their differences before they could come to agreements and create the world. They discov-ered that acknowledging their differences might not be an obstacle to a common project but, rather, the very foundation upon which the world could be created. At a time when so many different people had stood up in solidarity with Acteal and the Zapatistas, was it equally possible that those differences across national boundaries, languages, cultures, skin color, etc. could provide the basis for the constitution of a global movement for a better world?

If we return to our story, those seven mythic gods very likely find an echo in the seven historical constituent groups of the Zapatista movement: Tzotzil, Tzeltal, Tojolabal, Chol, Mame, Zoque, and mestizo. These "gods" at the origin of the EZLN came to grasp that they were different from one another. Six Mayan ethnic groups and one group of mestizos understood that these differences enriched them, and that by recognizing them they were all made stronger. It was then that the seven groups created the Zapatista world. If they could do it, perhaps today communicating with multiple others elsewhere will lead to the creation of a bigger project still, that of a world "where many worlds fit."

Coda

The old paramilitary structures of the 1990s remain intact as we write this in the 2020s. Not a single weapon was ever confiscated, and some of the very perpetrators of the Acteal massacre are still present in the renamed paramilitary groups that have again been carrying out raids in the region. As recently as November 18, 2020, paramilitaries attacked a caravan bringing humanitarian aid to refugees in Zapatista communities. Catholic clergy and human rights groups warn of the imminence of "another Acteal." The López Obrador government recently brokered a "peace agreement" with a split-away sector of the families of Acteal, but it once again failed to dismantle the paramilitaries—or repudiate their counterinsurgency purpose.[3] As Hermann Bellinghausen writes, "Governments may come and go, but the counterinsurgency war against the Indigenous communities of Chiapas never ends, and judging by the events of recent months in the mountains of the Mayan territories, in 2020, violence has worsened to a degree not seen in years."[4]

At a moment when repression in Chiapas has intensified, the Zapatistas again refuse to be encircled and, in a wholly unexpected move, as we mentioned in our previous commentary, have planned an intercontinental expedition. Since so many sympathizers protested after Acteal and have come to Chiapas since the uprising to share the Zapatistas' struggle, this time the Zapatistas will go to visit them, to learn about their worlds through their struggles. In their recent communiqués,[5] they mention some of the projected stops on their visit and, in the process, reveal an "Other Europe" to all of us: the Saami people, historically reindeer shepherds, whose territory is divided among Norway, Sweden, Finland, and Russia, and who are in a struggle against dispossession by extraction and the construction of a high-speed "Arctic Train" meant to spur commerce between Europe and Asia; the "No Tap" activists in Italy, who oppose the construction of the Trans Adriatic Pipeline, designed to carry gas from Azerbaijan to Europe to the detriment of local communities; the activists in Notre-Dame-des-Landes, in France, who oppose an airport and have established a *Zone à Défendre* (ZAD) that has become a referent for other struggles. The list is long.[6]

An End to the War of Extermination

How to kill a lion without a firearm.

"The Story of the Lion and the Mirror" appears in the communiqué "Above and Below: Masks and Silences" that broke more than four months of silence by the General Command of the EZLN and Subcomandante Marcos. Rumors of Marcos's death, illness, and assassination abounded during this time, including in an article in the *New York Times* that reported he was dying of malaria. Ironically, this period of "silence" coincides with frequent communiqués issued by the Zapatista autonomous communities themselves.[1] On more than a hundred occasions, they denounced military and paramilitary attacks, but it seemed no one was listening—as if only Marcos was of interest to the government and the media. The *comandancia*'s last communiqués had been issued in early March 1998, following the second anniversary of the signing of the San Andrés Accords. At that time, an exasperated Marcos repeated his charges of a year earlier that the accords were only a marketing stunt, and that the government had never intended to implement them. Indeed, he was proved right. President Zedillo would submit a counterproposal to the accords to the Congress—a revised version that was never approved by the EZLN or the communities, leading to the Zapatistas' charge of another betrayal and bad faith. Clearly, there was no point to further dialogue. The period of silence by the comandancia and Marcos ensued.

With all talks with the government suspended and constant military incursions, the Zapatista communities were tense. The response of the EZLN leadership to that tension was to insist that the communities not succumb to the government's constant provocations to fight each other, even if, as Marcos put it, "you have to run away to the hills, leaving behind what little you have."[2] Furthermore, by June, Samuel Ruiz, Bishop of San Cristóbal de las Casas,[3] had resigned from the commission that mediated between the government and the Zapatistas, leading to the commission's dissolution and the end of official channels of communication between the government and the EZLN. These were never resumed.

This disturbing story of animals' hearts ripped out and a lion's mouth torn apart by rusted nails and broken mirrors initially shocked us with its raw violence. Investigating its context, we discovered how brutal and constant the government's assaults on the Zapatista communities had been throughout 1998, a year, Mariana Mora tells us, that is engraved in the local memory of Chiapas, due to the extreme violence of state repression aimed at destroying the autonomous communities and punishing them for "usurping authority."[4] In a prior communiqué issued immediately after the Acteal massacre in December 1997, the Sup had detailed the counterinsurgency apparatus deployed in Chiapas, which included soldiers trained by the notoriously fascistic *Kaibiles* of Guatemala and "the same bullets used in Vietnam." More than a hundred army incursions were recorded in as many Zapatista communities in just the first three months of 1998. We focus on two such events that are emblematic of the lion's assault on the communities— and their resistance.

The first of these events, among so many, occurred in a small hamlet, X'oyep, in the municipality of Chenalhó. On January 2, 1998, soldiers invaded the community and took

Chenalhó, Chiapas, January 3, 1998. A group of women demanding that soldiers get out of the camp where they had sought refuge after the Acteal massacre. Photograph: Pedro Valtierra

possession of the spring that served as the sole water source for the thirteen resident families and the more than one thousand refugees,[5] including newcomers from the Acteal tragedy that those families had given asylum to. By depriving them of water, the army hoped to force those displaced people to migrate or disperse (again!). The next morning, however, after an urgent *asamblea*, the community of refugees took action and furiously confronted the soldiers, demanding they leave. Led by the women, they accosted, screamed at, and even slapped the soldiers, who after four hours of clashes were forced to pull out. A photo, "The Women of X'oyep," taken by photographer Pedro Valtierra and published in *La Jornada* the following morning, became and remains an icon of the Chiapas resistance.

What we see in the photo is women attacking with their bare hands. They appear resolute, fearless, and indignant. The big soldier in the foreground of the picture is made to seem bigger, perhaps by the camera angle, but certainly in contrast to the arms and size of the two women who are pushing him away. Yet he seems unsettled as he draws back, while another soldier must support him so that he doesn't fall. His imbalance and the powerful agency of the women become, for a moment, a symbol of an old order about to topple. For the duration of that shutter speed at least, we can imagine that "another world is possible."

The second event that we will mention here is the attack on the town of Taniperla that occurred four months later, on April 11, 1998. The Zapatista bases of support had declared Taniperla the municipal seat of their new Autonomous Rebel Municipality of Ricardo Flores Magón.[6] To celebrate its inauguration, they painted a mural on the newly built *casa munici-pal*, portraying in the foreground idyllic scenes of community life as they dreamed it and, in the background, the Zapatista protectors on the mountains that overlook the communities in resistance. The morning after its inauguration, the Mexican army destroyed the mural hoping to erase this singular vision of the Zapatista utopia. Painter Sergio Valdez Ruvalcaba, who organized the collective work of designing and painting the mural, describes the operation: "1200 soldiers arrived in fifty trucks, from all the police forces of the state, the federal police, immigration, and the army. Twelve hundred soldiers invading a community of barely 2500 people, no? ... It was a very effective theater of terror: they burned down houses, a community kitchen, an auditorium that had been recently built by the Zapatistas. And obviously the mural was a target of this repression."[7]

However, soon after its destruction, the mural was reproduced—like a refracting mirror—in many places around the world, more than forty-six of them from San Francisco to La Plata, Barcelona, Toronto, and elsewhere.[8] When a new administrative center for Flores Magón was reconstructed in 2005 in the town of *La Culebra*, so too was the mural. Here again, internationalism was of the essence—the Spanish National Workers Confederation and the Greek collective "A School for Chiapas" both contributed to the reconstruction.

The brutality of "The Story of the Lion and the Mirror" refracts the violence of this historical moment. The lion, intoxicated by the taste of blood, mistakes his own blood for that of the calf he wants to devour and ends up bleeding to death. We wondered if this story is perhaps a parable about how counterinsurgency fails: thinking it is consuming the blood of its enemy, the state bleeds itself out. As Zapatista support bases and allies articulated so movingly in *Fuerte Es Su Corazón*, "We are not in the buildings they destroyed but, rather, in every milpa and pasture,[9] in every river and mountain path, in every house and community of those of us who have a true heart, those of us who respect our different brother.... [T]hey can destroy our buildings, persecute our council, make us prisoners, charge us with a thousand crimes, and even kill us. But how will they stifle our will and desire for a future that is already ours?"[10] The buildings and murals are only the shell of the communities' resistance. As the state loses legitimacy, the strength of the Zapatistas grows in the *true heart* of the people.

As the Zapatistas conclude that the possibility of negotiating with the government is dead, they will again turn to civil society to propose a second national *consulta*, a plebiscite for or against the San Andrés Accords and for an end to the war of extermination. This proposal is the subject of the Fifth Declaration of the Lacandon Jungle, sent along with the communiqué in which "The Story of the Lion and the Mirror" appears. The EZLN's silence was broken.

Actually, it had been broken two days before with the release of two very fleeting communiqués. The first one, defiant and funny, is addressed to the cabal of forces arrayed against the Zapatistas: the Mexican army, the Guatemalan army, the Interpol in France, and the Mexican intelligence agency. Its irreverent message to these forces is a mocking: "Giddy up, giddy up, giddy up, *ándale, ándale*," signed by El Sup Speedy González. The second, written in Nahuatl, and addressed to Mexicans from below, is meant to remind them that Zapata lives on: "*Nemi Zapata*"!

A Matter of Time

This playful story was issued on the same day as two angry communiqués denouncing the government's response to a summer and fall of torrential rains and devastating floods throughout Chiapas—made worse by deforestation, corruption, and neglect. Indeed, as the Sup charges in these documents, the magnitude of their environmental tragedy is not due solely to a climate event; rather, it is the incapacity of the government of Chiapas to act in the face of natural disasters and the corruption of those in power that multiplied the destructive effects of the rains. When it became apparent that the interim governor of Chiapas was pocketing a good deal of the aid destined for flood victims, the *comandancia* recalled the fate of Anastasio Somoza who famously appropriated the humanitarian aid sent to Nicaragua following the 1975 earthquake—a prelude to his overthrow by the Sandinistas. Yet even as the outlook continued to darken, the Sup wrote this whimsical tale. In it, as indeed in most stories in our collection, Marcos's playfulness is notable. His humor is unconventional within the political domain, certainly within leftist politics. The language, the word plays, the multiple "times" are dizzying—and hard to translate!

Here, the Zapatistas celebrate *One Time* and *Another Time*, nuisances that interrupt the empire of *Forever* (the same) and *Never* (anything different). These last two seem to be a reference

to the PRI—the single political party that, albeit under different names, had been in power for more than seventy years
since the end of the Mexican Revolution. As Marcos points
out in an earlier communiqué, the PRI in Chiapas continues
to steal, as Always, and, as Always, distributes resources to
those in desperate need only in exchange for votes, whereas
the Zapatistas promise to share what little they have with the
flood victims—be they Zapatistas or not. After the floods, after
the massacres at Acteal, Chavajeval, and Unión Progreso,[1] after
the onslaught on the autonomous municipalities throughout
the year, just when it seems hopeless to resist, the Zapatistas
come from below, One Time and Another Time, to remind us
that every social order is open to becoming [something] better.

On Autonomous Education

"The Story of Looking" was read as a welcome to a meeting of teachers and students from Mexico's National Pedagogical University and its rural teacher-training colleges, or "normal schools." Throughout August, many other teachers and students came to Chiapas—all fighting the unfolding neoliberal assault on education. This meeting took place in the autonomous community of La Realidad. The Sup took advantage of the unlikely name to welcome the visitors to *La Realidad Mexicana*—where these spaces of democratic encounter were nearly encircled by the expanding presence of the army. With army and police checkpoints every ten kilometers to harass them, conflict with the Zapatista communities was ensured. When it did break out on August 12, the students and teachers assembled in La Realidad walked for twelve hours to the remote village of Amador Hernández to join the Zapatistas in defending their community. The threat and tension were so high that Marcos went offline soon after, not to reappear again until August 31, when he addressed those gathered again at La Realidad for a meeting "In Defense of our Culture and Heritage."[1]

In the full communiqué in which this story is embedded, Marcos begins his welcome to teachers and would-be teachers by recalling his own most important teacher—the figure he calls Old Antonio. This great teacher, he tells them, never finished elementary school and perhaps learned to read and write from those first gods who populate his stories. Many of the early members of the Zapatista organization did, in fact, learn to read, write, and speak Spanish through their organizing experiences, not in school. State public education barely reached the Indigenous communities of Chiapas.[2] Where it did, it was about erasure, demeaning their being as Indigenous— backward but redeemable through assimilation into a unified mestizo nation. The communities, however, had their own modes of education, transmitted orally, often through storytelling.[3] The tales of Old Antonio, for example, which come out of that other educational legacy, combine long cultural memory with the analysis of radical campesino struggles.

Since 1994, the Zapatista communities have refused government schoolteachers, instead constructing an autonomous education system that has been a central project throughout Zapatista territory. Today, most Zapatista communities have their own primary school, there is at least one full-fledged secondary school in Oventic, and since the formation of the first five caracoles in 2003 each autonomous region offers some form of post-primary training for health and education promoters. With the August 2019 announcement of seven more caracoles,[4] more autonomous schools will likely be popping up throughout Chiapas, and even a university has been added to the Zapatista organization. It is significant that the autonomous secondary schools function on a schedule tied to the demands of working on the milpa. Students return to their communities biweekly, reflecting the Zapatistas' understanding of the multiple sites and forms of education that are not apart from but integral to the production of life.

Every school in Zapatista territory is autonomous, that is to say, has its own way of looking and of looking at others looking. One of the aspirations throughout the autonomous schools is a revitalization of their local Indigenous traditions and languages that were suppressed and derided in the government schools. The autonomous schools do include some of the same subjects as state education, but for their own ends: Spanish, for example, is not taught as a replacement for the local language, and mathematics is not taught for job skills in the capitalist economy. Aside from their intrinsic value, these subjects are understood as tools to prevent being taken advantage of and swindled in the Spanish-speaking cities and to learn how to do accounting for the autonomous cooperatives. Could this mode of incorporation be one form of looking at the other looking? Could the story also be a message to the teachers and future teachers in the audience, to learn to see the world as their students see it, so they don't "bump into them, hurt, step over, or trip them"?

The power of the gaze here also recalls Du Bois's "double-consciousness" and Frantz Fanon's "Look, a Negro!"[5] both meditations on the Black experience of being objectified, suddenly made aware of how you are seen by powerful, contemptuous—or frightened—others. The story pivots to a transmutation of that oppressive double consciousness into something like a "second sight," the perspective of those "from below and to the left" who understand that different others see the world differently, and that to move forward at all they must recognize each other's different ways of seeing and experiencing the world.

Returning to our story, we recall the image with which it begins, which could so easily go unnoticed: "A spiral of smoke slowly leaves Old Antonio's mouth. Contemplating it, he begins to shape it into sign and word." This transmutation of a spiral of smoke into the word is an allusion to pre-Columbian Mesoamerican art. Both in codices (pictographic manuscripts) and in stele (carved stone monuments), certain figures are accompanied by speech scrolls, curlicues of smoke that usually reference the person's function—poet, painter, king, teacher—or in our earliest illustration below, musicians. This motif of the speech scroll, preserved as cultural memory for centuries, is now found in contemporary murals painted in the Zapatista communities.

Below are two ancient images: the first from the Codex Borbonicus, exemplifying pre-Columbian aesthetics; the second, a later representation from the Florentine Codex. The subsequent images are from Zapatista communities.

Two Gods Singing, page 4 of the Aztec *Codex Borbonicus* (sixteenth century).

"Listening to the Admonitions of the Elders," *Florentine Codex*, Book 9 (sixteenth century). From "Is There a Name for the Aztec Speech Glyph?" *Mexicolore* Pic. 4

Mural on the wall of a video equipment house for the Chiapas Media Project. Photo by Mary Watkins, Oventic, Chiapas, 2003

Recording the world in Oventic, Chiapas. Photo by Mary Watkins, Oventic, Chiapas, 2003

The Zapatista Legacy

"We Who Came After Did Understand" was read by Subcomandante Marcos in La Realidad on August 31, 1999, at the closing of the "National Meeting in Defense of Our Cultural Heritage." This event was attended by members of Mexico's National Institute and National School of Anthropology and History. It was these anthropology students and teachers, Marcos tells us, who had alerted the Zapatistas about a government bill planning to "auction off" Mexico's cultural patrimony. They had come to La Realidad to join forces with the Zapatistas, along with UNAM students on strike, members of the dissident teachers' union, and electrical workers defending their union and the publicly owned utility. All were opposed to the neoliberal privatization of public institutions—institutions rooted in the national project of the Mexican Revolution: Indigenous communal lands and ejidos (1917 Constitution),[1] the national public university, the UNAM (founded in 1910); the INAH, the institution in charge of the protection of the nation's cultural heritage (founded by President Cárdenas in 1939), and the electrical workers union, and the SME (founded in 1914).[2] The demands of all these groups found echoes in the words of this UNAM student explaining their strike: "For us, education is not a commodity; it is one of the social rights we won in Mexico."[3] *Education* could be replaced here by *cultural patrimony* or *electricity*. Or by *land*, considering that, as Marcos reminds us,

"When Mexican government officials say *land*, they precede the word with an 'I buy' or 'I sell,' since for the powerful land is just a commodity. When the Indigenous say *land*, no word precedes it, but with it they also mean *nation, mother, home, school, history, wisdom*."[4] The struggle over the significance and survival of these concepts, in opposition to the economic rationality of neoliberalism, is at the heart of our story.

The man who planted trees was made fun of for being so impractical: "Why do you work on things that you will never see finished?" his neighbors asked mockingly. But others understand, as they rescue those dreams from the past—Zapata's dreams, for example—and refuse their descent into oblivion. Once the trees have grown and are full of birds, they bring joy and shade to a new generation, who in turn send a message back to the madman in the past.

In real life, the *trees* were perhaps those planted thirty years earlier, in another August, "the month of memory."[5] With this phrase Marcos alludes to the founding, on August 6, 1969, in distant Monterrey, of the organization that would become the predecessor of the EZLN: the Forces of National Liberation (FLN).[6] Even though many of its members were killed in the seventies and eighties, the seeds of the FLN from the north of Mexico reached the Zapatista south, and either as a result of that bridge, or perhaps from the preexistence of Indigenous activism in Chiapas, or a mixture of everything, Zapatismo turned out creative, unpredictable, and not easy to define.

That unpredictability, or protean resiliency, is illustrated by the following examples. In 2001, after the March of the Color of the Earth from Chiapas to Mexico City, expecting Congress to implement the San Andrés Accords, the Zapatistas experienced another betrayal. Their hopes were shattered by yet another president, Vicente Fox (2000–2006), and, in fact, by all of the political parties. When their autonomy was not formally recognized, they surprised both friends and enemies by declaring their de facto autonomy, founding five caracoles,[7] regional governments that link and organize networks of Zapatista autonomous municipalities (see map below).[8] Fifteen years later, in 2019, they breached the government siege and formed seven more caracoles, four autonomous municipalities, and something new: "Centers for Autonomous Resistance and Zapatista Rebellion."[9]

Since 2001, the Zapatistas pivoted decisively away from the state to strengthen their internal organization and eventually build a broader movement with all those like themselves, from below and to the left. This was announced in the "Sixth Declaration of the Lacandon Jungle," known thenceforth as the "Sexta" (Sixth). They embarked on the "Other Campaign," a project to acquaint themselves with all those left out or ignored by neoliberalism and invite them to join forces to change the world. It was while traveling through Mexico in 2006, in this campaign of solidarity and listening to others that Marcos visited the small museum that memorializes the origin of the FLN and the EZLN, the Casa-Museo del Dr. Margil in Monterrey.[10] He arrived there on November 17, 2006, to celebrate the anniversary of the founding of the EZLN on that date in 1983. But in upside-down Zapatista style, he celebrated the ancestors instead: he recalled the founders, the founders' parents, and all those who have since died in the struggle—among whom he names "El compañero Mario Marcos, native of Monterrey, Nuevo León, fallen in the course of duty in 1982, and whose name I now bear."[11] He honors the men and women of the 1960s, 1970s, and 1980s, the "generation of dignity," those who "left everything to have nothing .... [T]he generation whose dream was to give birth to us and pass on the best of their personal and collective history."

Acknowledging to his audience that many puzzle over what it is that the Zapatistas want, the Sup replied calmly to that question: to sow the tree of the future, that's what they want. And he further elaborated that, as crazy as it may sound, it's not only what they want, it's what they do.

The First Five *Caracoles*, 2003

Some Room Left for Love and Poetry

This story appears in a letter, "Insurgentas! La Mar en marzo," numbered 6.e., written by Subcomandante Marcos on March 8, 2000, the last in a series of letters he had been writing since the beginning of the year. The first letter, 6.a., was to the poet Juan Gelman, who was at that point searching for his missing grandchild, whose parents had been disappeared by the Argentine military. Three other letters (6.b.–6.d.) addressed Mexican figures who had been steadfast on the side of the Zapatistas: a historian of Mexico's Indigenous populations; a courageous university rector who defended striking students against the army; and a musician. Why are these letters linked in a series? Marcos challenges his readers to find the connections. All of those addressed are individual rebels who fight—with music, history, poetry—against both bullets and *el olvido*, the erasure or dismissal of histories, struggles, memories. Until, that is, we arrive at 6.e. This letter is addressed to a collective subject, the *insurgentas*—women soldiers—on International Women's Day 2000. It honors their remarkable contribution to the struggle, especially in their roles as combatants and troop commanders. Marcos calls particular attention to men's initial pushback against following women's orders in combat, an attitude lessened somewhat by the women's bravery and intelligence during the uprising—but not by any means, he tells us, eliminated. In a communiqué issued on another International

Women's Day, in 1996, Marcos points to the irony that at the very moment when Major Ana María, an Indigenous woman, has captured a city—San Cristóbal, on January 1, 1994—she and all Zapatista women are again pushed into the background, made invisible by the media's fascination with him—the fair-skinned one behind the ski mask. The Zapatista struggle, distinctively, incorporated women at its center from the beginning, and officially from the moment in which the Women's Revolutionary Law was adopted in March of 1993. The "first uprising of the EZLN," Marcos called it, was led by women, and in which, despite resistance from the men, "there were no casualties, and the women won."[1] The participation of women underlies the strength of the entire Zapatista project and provides the ongoing momentum to challenge the inherited hierarchies of the state and the communities.[2]

The letter "6.e." pays tribute to one woman in particular, La Mar, the woman Marcos loves and who now seems distant. We learn that she designed, anonymously, the Zapatista referendum on Indigenous rights held one year before, mobilizing over five thousand representatives to travel around the country and organize the vote. Unsurprisingly, perhaps, but invisibly, the plebiscite itself was implemented mostly by women. The narration shifts from La Mar to Durito, who Marcos turns to for advice in the midst of his lovesickness. Durito tells him the only recourse is to cast a spell—to remind her of a time, not when they looked into each-others' eyes, but when they looked toward the future together. We don't know if La Mar accepts the spell, but the Sup shares the memory he offered her in "The Story of the Night Air."

"The Story of the Night Air" is another foundation narrative, in which the gods create the world. What they create, specifically, are not singular components of our world as in the biblical story but, instead, micro-environments of collaboration or synergy: the air and birds together or water and fish together or man and woman together.[3] In stark contrast, however, there is an individual who rebels against this arrangement: it is tzotz (bat), who complains about the limitations the air imposes on his flight. Angered by his dissatisfaction, the gods punish him ruthlessly by blinding him and removing his feathers. Now defenseless and alone, "naked and blind," thrust eyeless into existence, the bat learns to orient itself by talking to things of the world, whose answers it alone can understand. The rebellious tzotz has thus been transfigured into a poet, a blind seer like Homer, Milton, Borges, who through words brings forth worlds from the night that surrounds us.

A poet—or a Zapatista—since it was from this bird, the tzotz, that "the true men and women learned to recognize the greatness and power of the spoken word, the sound of thought." In their assemblies, indeed, the Zapatistas orient themselves precisely by speaking and listening to each other, sending out, receiving, and interpreting words. They do this until they create worlds in the night, just like the first gods did in this story—or like those earlier men, women, and "eight children capable of reasoning" had done in 1992 in the town of the two Antonios in our first story.

Afterword

The calendar? An early morning in April. Geography? The mountains of the Mexican Southeast. A sudden silence overtakes the crickets, the distant barking of dogs, and the echo of marimba music...

The mountain gets up, shyly lifting her skirts a bit and, not without some difficulty, pulls her feet out of the earth. She takes a first step, grimacing in pain. Far from maps, tourist destinations and catastrophes, the soles of the small mountain's feet are bleeding. But here all are in on the plan, so an unexpected rain falls to wash her feet and cure her wounds.

"Take care, daughter," says the mother Ceiba tree. "You can do it!" says the Huapác tree, as if to itself. The pauraque bird leads the way. "Go east, friend, go east," it says as it hops from side to side. Clothed in trees, birds, and stones, the mountain walks, and with each step, sleepy men, women, persons who are neither men nor women, and boys and girls grab onto her skirts. They climb up her blouse, crown the tip of her breasts, continue up her shoulders, and, when they have reached the top of her head, they awaken.

To the east, the sun, just edging above the horizon, slows its stubborn daily rise. It's quite a sight to see a mountain, with a crown of humans, walking along. But besides the sun and a few gray clouds that the night left behind, no one here seems surprised.

"So it was written," says Old Antonio.[1]

This is a tender depiction, like a child's drawing perhaps, of the departure of "Squadron 421" from Chiapas to Europe. In times like ours, when tourism and catastrophe stalk our daily jumble of news and advertising, this is a reminder of how it once was long ago and of the meaning of territory—that which will carry the Zapatistas, like a mother, on their intercontinental trip for life. When it was announced in the midst of a pandemic, the global tour seemed like an improbable Zapatista "delirium," as Marcos/Galeano himself labeled it, but not only did it materialize, it has now been completed. It started when the seven members of "Squadron 421" arrived in Galicia, Spain, on June 22, 2021, on a German sailboat built in 1904. It continued with the arrival of roughly 170 members of the airborne delegation, "La Extemporánea,"[2] in Vienna, on September 14 and 15, and concluded with a note on December 12 from Subcomandante Moisés, the coordinator of the European journey, thanking all their new friends and hosts. "La Extemporánea" was joined by members of the governing council of the National Indigenous Congress, including their spokesperson and former presidential candidate Marichuy, as well as members of the Morelos-Puebla-Tlaxcala Peoples' Front in Defense of Land and Water.

Of those seven months, two early events seem particularly resonant with symbolism. The first is the initial anchoring and descent at the port of Baiona—where 528 years earlier the caravel *La Pinta* had arrived, bringing back the first news of Columbus's "discovery." Here, as noted in the introduction to our collection, Marijose replicates the acts of the early conquistadors, but in reverse, since it is now the Indigenous who do the renaming, Europe becoming *Slumil K'ajxemk'op*, Land of the Insubordinate.[3]

This initiates a process of resignification, amplified on August 13, 2021, at a rally in Madrid, when some two thousand "insubordinate" Europeans marched to the Plaza Colón (Columbus Square), the emblematic center of present-day Spanish ultraright political parties. The Zapatistas themselves rode to that plaza in a colorful float representing their ship, with a banner proclaiming: "You did not conquer us!" On the very day of the five hundredth anniversary of the fall of Mexico-Tenochtitlán, these Zapatistas were not protesting the conquest as much as celebrating the birth of their resistance. Their speeches to the crowd were promptly posted that evening on Enlace Zapatista in a document titled: "Only 500 Years Later."[4]

The Zapatistas went to Europe to meet those others who, like them, work to create autonomous forms of life that reject the depredations of capitalism. Their expedition's motto, "For Life," indicates that its mission remains untethered from an exclusively, or exclusionary, Indigenous cause; without abandoning it, they continue to seek broader alliances to oppose the dispossession of territories and the destruction of the planet. Their analyses of the sinister procedures that are put in motion to redirect the world economy are down to earth and conceptually useful in multiple situations in our present. Thus, for example, the Ukrainian journalist Oleg Yasinsky, in an analysis of his country's current situation, resorts to quoting the Zapatistas as follows:

> According to Zapatista analysis, there are at present two stages in the capitalist conquest of new territories: the first consists of the ... depopulation of the enemy territory, and the second of the ... reordering of the conquered land to suit the interests of the new owner. Petro Poroshenko [former President of Ukraine, 2014–2019] was involved in the dirtiest part of the war, which served as an ... alibi for the destruction of the

country's industry, science, education, and health, laying their still smoldering ruins at the feet of their new masters. Volodymyr Zelensky has been in charge of what followed: ... an anti-agrarian reform enabling corporations to privatize the land; technological and IT advances to put the country at the service of international financial flows; the entry of the transnationals; the destruction of any critical communication media; and the final legal touch-ups to consolidate total control and make irreversible the domination of the country by foreign capital.[5]

In the case of the Zapatistas, and more broadly the numerous Indigenous groups in Mexico that struggle to protect their territory, the two stages can overlap. The first violent stage of capitalist destruction today is still carried out by paramilitaries: present since 1994, notorious worldwide since Acteal, they have continued to murder with equal impunity and better weapons until the present. The goal appears to be to free the area of its inhabitants. When the Zapatistas in Chiapas and their allies in Oaxaca, Morelos, and other places reject the current government's megaprojects, they are saying no to loss of territory, the link of land and culture. Metaphorically speaking, Zapatistas fight to avoid the destruction of that shy and powerful maternal mountain that marches at dawn with her people toward the sea.

This confrontation with megaprojects finds echoes in the situation of the Sami people from the northern regions of Norway, Sweden, Finland, and the Kola Peninsula in Russia, who are among the only Indigenous people in the European Union. The Zapatistas visited them in Kola, in September 2021.[6] While the Zapatistas have been opposing the "Mayan Train" through Indigenous lands,[7] the Sami have been fighting the construction of the Arctic Railway they fear will split their territory in half—a territory already separated by the borders of four different states. The train will kill many of the reindeer that the Sami herd, which constitute for many of them their only sustenance and income, and will attract a flurry of mining companies. According to Finnish climate scientist Tero Mustonen, "It is a bonanza. It is California 1848. It is a gold rush." In 2021, Finland was ranked as the best place to invest in mining and exploration.[8]

The Zapatistas also visited non-Indigenous groups in similar struggles against the corporate invasion of their territories. In late July, "Squadron 421" visited the ZAD (Zone à défendre, or Zone to Defend) in Notre-Dame-des-Landes, France, occupied in 2008 in defense against an airport megaproject. The occupiers are still there, even though the government has tried to evict them, and the airport project was canceled in 2018.[9] During these years of resistance, they visited and consulted with the Zapatista-allied Frente de Pueblos en Defensa de la Tierra (Peoples' Front in Defense of Land) in San Salvador Atenco, which fought its own struggle against the construction of a mega-airport in Mexico.[10] The Zapatistas were invited to the ZAD for a unique encounter: two days dedicated to discussions and art open only to women and gender dissidents; the third day included cis men. This is the first such event in Europe.[11]

Among the innumerable encounters between smaller delegations of Zapatistas and Europe in resistance, we mention only two. On September 25, 2021, a delegation of Kurdish women activists met in Frankfurt with Zapatista women to exchange information about their respective struggles to "resist capitalism, liberate women and build autonomy."[12] In both places, radical changes in gender relations are occurring in a context of tremendous violence and both high-and low-intensity war.[13] A month later, on October 22, 2021, the Zapatistas were invited to Galway, Ireland, where they saw a documentary about recovering women, who in 2000 had reproduced the mural "Life and Dreams in the Canyons of Taniperla" as part of their healing process. Muireann de Barra's film *Muralistas* documents that process.[14] In a most moving encounter, the director and some of the now older painters saw the film again, eleven years later, this time in the company of their visitors from Chiapas.

This is a synopsis of a few highlights of the trip, a glimpse of international "territories" to which the Zapatistas have served as guides and a referent. It is our hope that there will soon be studies, reports, documentaries, theories, and, of course, communiqués, sharing the Zapatistas' experiences and the significance of these months abroad. Already an ever-growing website documenting the journey for life, *Al Faro Zapatista*, has been created by social scientists turned activists by the Zapatista dream.[15]

In a 1999 story,[16] Durito himself narrates his trip to many of those same places in Europe—Italy, England, Denmark, Germany, France, Geneva, Holland, Belgium, Sweden, the Iberian Peninsula, the Canary Islands, all of Europe—from where he comes back transformed into a pirate. The day of his return was none other than October 12, and Durito, now "Black Shield," demands to know the name of the Caribbean island where he has just found Marcos. Confused, Marcos, who is sitting on top of a ceiba tree, not on any island, finally says, "It has no name." Durito finds this a dignified name for a pirate's island and proclaims: "On today's date, October 12, 1999, I pronounce to have discovered, conquered, and liberated this island called 'it has no name.'" As a last question we ask ourselves: Have Marcos and Durito been dreaming of the Zapatista trip ever since? Did Marijose learn from Durito the formula for their address to the people in Baiona? Have the members of "Squadron 421" and "La Extemporánea" also transformed into pirates?

Notes

Introduction to the English Translation of *Los Otros Cuentos*

1   Elaine Katzenberger, ed., *First World, Ha Ha Ha! The Zapatista Challenge* (San Francisco: City Lights, 1995); a collection of Zapatista writings in English that took as its title the slogan of one of the early pro-Zapatista marches in Mexico.

2   Andrew Kopkind, "Opening Shots" (editorial), *Nation* 258, no. 4 (January 31, 1994); quoted in Tom Hayden, ed., *The Zapatista Reader* (New York: Thunder's Mouth Press/Nation Books, 2002), 19–21.

3   Soon identified as EZLN Subcomandante Marcos, or "the Sup," as he is affectionately known.

4   Paulina Fernández summarizes the power relations of life on the fincas, where "[t]he *finquero* derives his power over the field peons through property in land. Owning the land makes him the owner of their labor. Since their labor power is the only thing the peons, their wives and children have, the landowner considers himself the owner of their life as well, and he forces his peons to understand this in every moment of every day"; see Paulina Fernández Christlieb, *Justicia Autónoma Zapatista, Zona Tzeltal* (Mexico: Estampa/Ediciones Autónom@s, 2014), 50.

5   David Harvey, *A Brief History of Neoliberalism* (New York: Oxford University Press, 2007) remains the classic Marxist analysis of neoliberalism as a class project to restore the power and wealth of capital against labor. For Harvey's recent take, see "The Neoliberal Project Is Alive but Has Lost Its Legitimacy," Wire, February 9, 2019, accessed October 3, 2021, https://thewire.in/economy/david-harvey-marxist-scholar-neo-liberalism.

6   According to Florencia Mallon, in the project of nation-state formation in independent Latin America, Indigenous visions of inclusion with autonomy were everywhere rejected in favor of a European "one size fits all" liberal notion of individual citizenship that today is

being challenged by Indigenous movements throughout the region; see "Indigenous Peoples and Nation States in 1780–2000," José C. Moya, ed., *The Oxford Handbook of Latin American History* (New York: Oxford University Press, 2011); for a related US discussion, see Miguel Salazar, "The Problem with Latinidad," *Nation*, September 16, 2019, accessed September 28, 2021, https://www.thenation.com/article/archive/hispanic-heritage-month-latinidad.

7　*Mestizo* (or mixed race) is Mexico's post-Revolutionary national identity/ideology. Above, it refers to non-Indigenous Mexicans, who in Chiapas, as in Guatemala, are also, and perhaps more commonly, referred to as *ladinos*.

8　See Nicholas Higgins, "Visible Indians: Subcomandante Marcos and the Indianization of the EZLN," in *Understanding the Chiapas Rebellion: Modernist Visions and the Invisible Indian* (Austin: University of Texas Press, 2004), 153–71; Dylan Fitzwater, *Autonomy Is in Our Hearts: Zapatista Autonomous Government through the Lens of the Tsotsil Language* (Oakland: PM Press, 2019).

9　Those chosen to rule had to carry out the will of the community; their task was to rule by obeying, *mandar obedeciendo*.

10　This site in Scotland followed the Zapatistas' voyage to Europe; Scotland Zapatista, Twitter, accessed October 3, 2021, https://twitter.com/scotlandzapat/status/1406359329758928901?s=27; for a communiqué from a collective that spans Mexico City, Spain, and Germany, see Trenzando sueños y resistencias, accessed October 3, 2021, https://www.caminoalandar.org/post/trenzando-sue%C3%B1os-y-resistencias.

11　A wonderful Spanish-language documentary follows the campaign; Nicolas Défossé, dir., ¡*Viva Mexico!* (Chiapas, MX: Terra Nostra Films, 2010), accessed October 3, 2021, https://centroprodh.org.mx/sididh_2_0_alfa/?p=30799.

12　To read the "Sexta" in English, see "Zapatista Army of National Liberation," Enlace Zapatista, accessed October 3, 2021, https://enlacezapatista.ezln.org.mx/sdsl-en; it can also be found in Spanish on the Enlace Zapatista site, where all the communiqués are archived by date and sometimes include translations into English and other languages, see Enlace Zapatista, EZLN Documents (2012–2021), accessed September 28, 2021, http://enlacezapatista.ezln.org.mx/category/comunicado. Throughout this book, we use the Enlace site for all of the communiqués in Spanish.

13　You can see footage from the Silent March at "Zapatistas Silent Mobilization (December 21, 20120)," Dorset Chiapas Solidarity, December 25, 2012, accessed October 3, 2021, https://dorsetchiapassolidarity.wordpress.com/2012/12/25/zapatistas-silent-mobilization-december-21-2012.

14 For a reflection on the Little School, see Raúl Zibechi, "The Schools from Below," *In Motion Magazine*, September 15, 2013, accessed September 28, 2021, https://inmotionmagazine.com/global/r_zibechi_escuelitas.html; originally published in *La Jornada*, August 23, 2013.

15 See Emily Keppler, "Another Government Is Possible," Intercontinental Cry, October 17, 2016, accessed October 3, 2021, https://intercontinentalcry.org/another-government-possible.

16 Juan Villoro, "Prohibido Votar por una Indígena," *New York Times* (Spanish edition), February 24, 2018, accessed September 28, 2021, https://www.nytimes.com/es/2018/02/24/espanol/opinion/opinion-villoro-marichuy.html.

17 See John Gibler, *I Couldn't Even Imagine They Would Kill Us: An Oral History of the Attacks against the Students of Ayotzinapa* (San Francisco: City Lights/Open Media Paperback, 2017).

18 See Enlace Zapatista, July 21, 2003, https://enlacezapatista.ezln.org.mx/2003/07/21/chiapas-la-treceava-estela-primera-parte-un-caracol.

19 See "Chiapas: la treceava estela. Primera parte: un carcol," Enlace Zapatista, July 21, 2003, accessed April 8, 2022, https://enlacezapatista.ezln.org.mx/2003/07/21/chiapas-la-treceava-estela-primera-parte-un-caracol.

20 Estimates range from a conservative 531 square miles to a much larger grab of 2,000 to 3,000 square miles. An additional 400 square miles were seized by other peasant organizations during the period of the uprising. Thanks to Stuart Schussler for compiling these figures for his dissertation in progress, which he kindly shared with us, and for underlining the significance of this large-scale expropriation of the *finqueros* of Chiapas as the material basis of Zapatista autonomy.

21 Mariana Mora, *Kuxlejal Politics: Indigenous Autonomy, Race and Decolonizing Research in Zapatista Communities* (Austin, Tx: University of Texas Press, 2017), 233.

22 The Mayan Train is a mega development project designed to bring mass tourism to the Yucatan Peninsula and Chiapas, areas where Mayan Indigenous peoples of many distinct ethnicities have lived since before the Conquest; see "Letter from the Zapatista Women to Women in Struggle Around the World," Enlace Zapatista, February 13, 2019, accessed April 8, 2022, https://tinyurl.com/446kp48m; Claudio Lomnitz, "The Mayan Train: The Zapatistas Are Right," Chiapas Support Committee, January 20, 2019, accessed April 8, 2022, https://chiapas-support.org/2019/01/20/the-maya-train-the-zapatistas-are-right.

23 Alberto Cortés, dir., *Corazon del Tiempo* (Mexico: IMCINE/Filomteca UNAM, 2009); Margaret Cerullo, "The Zapatistas' Other Politics: The Subjects of Autonomy," in David Fasenfest, ed., *Engaging Social Justice: Critical Studies of 21st Century Social Transformation* (Chicago: Haymarket Books, 2012 [2009]).

24 See Anya Briy, "Zapatistas at 26: Autonomy and Women's Liberation," Medium, March 31, 2020, accessed October 3, 2021, https://chepresente2016.medium.com/zapatistas-at-26-autonomy-and-womens-liberation-78426ab08c27.

25 See, e.g., Mariana Mora, *Kuxlejal Politics: Indigenous Autonomy, Race, and Decolonizing Research in Zapatista Communities* (Austin: University of Texas Press, 2017); Melissa Forbis, "'Never Again a Mexico Without Us': Gender, Indigenous Autonomy and Multiculturalism in Neoliberal Mexico" (PhD diss., University of Texas, 2008), accessed October 3, 2021, https://repositories.lib.utexas.edu/handle/2152/18324. For an account of women's centrality to the uprising and to the development of the Zapatista project, based almost wholly on *testimonios*, see Hillary Klein, *Compañeras: Zapatista Women's Stories* (New York: Seven Stories Press, 2015).

26 See Anya Briy, "Zapatistas at 26."

27 "Marcos" disappeared on stage in May 2014. The Zapatistas decided that his role as their main spokesperson had come to an end. He was reborn as Subcomandante Galeano, adopting the *nombre de lucha* of a Zapatista teacher, savagely murdered that month by paramilitaries. The practice of adopting the name of fallen comrades dates back at least to the Mexican Revolution, when José Doroteo Arango Arámbula took the name Pancho Villa in honor of a friend who had died in battle. According to "the Sup," "Marcos" is also the name of a fallen comrade; see commentary to "We Who Came After Did Understand" and "The Zapatista Legacy," this volume, pages 33–35; 78–81

28 See Faith S., "Suffrage, Liberation, and Checking Your Engine," blog of Toledo Lucas County Public Library, unavailable November 11, 2021, https://www.toledolibrary.org/blog/suffrage-liberation-and-checking-your-engine.

29 See the wonderful videos of Zapatista women's driving adventures available at "Del cuaderno de apuntes del Gato-Perro: Rumbo al Puy Ta Cuxlejaltic, el CompArte de Danza y el Segundo Encuentro Internacional de Mujeres qu Luchan," Enlace Zapatista, September 11, 2019, accessed October 3, 2021, https://tinyurl.com/mws47tz7. We owe these videos to the "Terci@s Compas," the Zapatistas' own autonomous media collective, which has documented the actions and activities of the movement since August 2014.

30   Luci Caballero and Verónica Gago, "The Political Invention of the Feminist Strike," March 23, 2021, accessed October 3, 2021, https://viewpointmag.com/2021/03/23/the-political-invention-of-the-feminist-strike.

31   See "We Don't Need Permission to Fight for Life: Zapatista Women Join the March 9 National Strike," Enlace Zapatista, March 1, 2020, accessed October 3, 2021, https://tinyurl.com/uxfznp6e.

32   To follow the progress of their voyage, see Enlace Zapatista, EZLN Documents (2012–2021), where most of the recent communiqués have been translated into English. We particularly recommend "Escuadrón 421," translated as "The 421st Squadron," Enlace Zapatista, April 20, 2021, accessed October 3, 2021, http://enlacezapatista.ezln.org.mx/2021/04/20/421st-squadron.

33   A video of Marijose greeting activists upon their arrival in Vigo can be found in "The Landing," Enlace Zapatista, June 30, 2021, accessed March 18, 2022, https://enlacezapatista.ezln.org.mx/2021/06/30/the-landing.

34   Subcomandante Marcos, *Los Otros Cuentos* (Buenos Aires: Red de Solidaridad Zapatista, 2008).

35   The collection was accompanied by a CD on which each story was read aloud by figures significant to their cultural and political context—writer Eduardo Galeano, Nora Cortinas, one of the grandmothers of the *Plaza de Mayo*, folksinger León Gieco, among others. They are all available on YouTube.

36   See Yvon Le Bot, *Subcomandante Marcos y el sueño zapatista* (Barcelona: Plaza y Janés, 1997), 153.

37   See Rubén Darío, "To Roosevelt" (1904), accessed October 3, 2021, https://tinyurl.com/533wbbt7.

38   Comandante Insugente Tacho, "Siete Mensajes durante la Ceremonia de Entrega del Bastón de Mando al Subcomandante Marcos," Enlace Zapatista, November 17, 1994, accessed October 3, 2021, https://tinyurl.com/ark3esu8.

39   See "On Moles, Lions, and Democracy," this volume, pages 48–52.

40   Carlos Lenkersdorf, *Los Hombres Verdaderos: Voces y Testimonios Tojolabales* (México D.F., Madrid: Siglo XXI, 1996).

Antonio's Dream and a Prophecy

1   For Spanish original, see Enlace Zapatista, EZLN Documents (2012–2021), accessed September 28, 2021, http://enlacezapatista.ezln.org.mx/category/comunicado; for the English translation, see "The Southeast in Two Winds a Storm and a Prophecy," Schools for Chiapas, accessed October 3, 2021, https://schoolsforchiapas.org/library/southeast-winds-storm-prophecy.

2   Quoted in Jan De Vos, *Vienen de Lejos los Torrentes: una Historia de Chiapas* (Tuxtla Gutiérrez, Chiapas, México: Consejo Estatal para las Culturas y las Artes de Chiapas, 2010), 242. De Vos was a Belgian historian turned devoted resident and historian of Chiapas. For more on Samuel Ruiz, see page 99, "An End to the War of Extermination," note 3.

3   The ejido, enshrined until 1992 in the Mexican Constitution, is a form of communal land tenure, wherein land rights—the right of *possession* but not ownership—are held by the community, not by individuals. Families might control individual plots for generations, but the land could not be bought or sold.

4   De Vos, *Vienen de Lejos los Torrentes*, 366–69.

5   Starting in the 1960s but accelerating in the 1970s and 1980s, tens of thousands of indigenous campesinos driven by economic desperation after literally centuries of radical land dispossession and serfdom on their ancestral lands were forced to migrate from other parts of Chiapas to the "national lands" of the Lacandon jungle. The new communities they formed in the Lacandon (an estimated thousand containing two hundred to three hundred inhabitants by the 1990s) were a principal base of militant peasant organizing in the 1970s and became one of the crucibles of Zapatismo. The role of the Catholic Church, under the influence of liberation theology, was critical in organizing these far-flung communities; see Jan Rus, Rosalva Aída Hernández Castillo, and Shannan L. Mattiace, eds., *Mayan Lives, Mayan Utopias: The Indigenous People of Chiapas and the Zapatista Rebellion* (New York: Rowman and Littlefield, 2003); John Womack, Jr., *Rebellion in Chiapas: An Historical Reader* (New York: New Press, 1999)

Durito and Zapata Do Remember

1   Ejido land titles were held in perpetuity by the community. Since the Mexican Revolution, groups of peasants, including the Indigenous who began settled the Lacandon jungle in the 1970s, could petition the government for recognition of their new territory as ejido land. By 1992, about half of the farmland in Mexico was in the form of ejidos. At the time of the constitutional reform, thousands of ejido petitions were still pending with the agrarian reform commission, some dating back generations. With the abolishment of land reform, communities lost all hope of receiving ejido status. This explanation of the ejido is adapted from the Mexico Solidarity Network website, unavailable October 3, 2021, http://mexicosolidarity.org/programs/alternativeeconomy/zapatismo/en.

2   "These constitutional revisions not only ended redistribution of land to the *ejidos* but also paved the way for mass transfer of rural

land from Indigenous communities to multinational food corporations"; for a deeper exploration of these changes and a historical reconstruction of the ejido's continuity with the pre-Columbian *calpullis*, see James J. Kelly, "Article 27 and Mexican Land Reform: The Legacy of Zapata's Dream," *Columbia Human Rights Law Review* 25 (1993–1994): 541–70.

3   Subcomandante Marcos, "The Fourth World War Has Begun," *Le Monde Diplomatique*, September 26, 1997, accessed October 3, 2021, https://mondediplo.com/1997/09/marcos.

4   An excellent book assembles the communiqués involving Durito up until the moment of its publication in 2005; see Subcomandante Marcos, *Conversations with Durito: Stories of the Zapatistas and Neoliberalism*, edited and introduced by Acción Zapatista Editorial Collective (Brooklyn: Autonomedia, 2005).

5   See Rubén Darío, "To Roosevelt" (1904), accessed October 3, 2021, https://tinyurl.com/533wbbt7.

On Moles, Lions, and Democracy

1   It is customary to speak of the seventy-year reign of the PRI—from 1929, when the Partido Nacional Revolucionario (PNR) was founded by Plutarco Elías Calles, until 2000, when it lost the presidency to Vicente Fox of the right-wing party, the Partido de Acción Nacional (PAN). What the notion of the "unbroken reign of a single party" obscures is that the Mexican Revolution was leftist—the 1917 constitution was the most progressive in the world at the time. After the interval of Lázaro Cárdenas (1934–1940), the party moved decidedly to the right.

2   Comité Clandestino Revolucionario Indígena—Comandancia General (General Command of the Clandestine Indigenous Revolutionary Committee).

3   "Al Pueblo de México: en Nuestros Sueños Hemos Visto Otro Mundo," Enlace Zapatista, March 1, 1994, accessed November 11, 2021, https://tinyurl.com/45jydajr; "Al Pueblo de México: el Diálogo de San Cristóbal fue Verdadero," Enlace Zapatista, March 1, 1994, accessed November 11, 2021, https://tinyurl.com/25jm9yf5.

4   Subcomandante Marcos, "Sobre el Asesinato de Colosio: Ellos … ¿Por Qué Tuvieron que Hacer Eso?" Enlace Zapatista, March 24, 1994, accessed October 3, 2021, https://tinyurl.com/rt3v2fz7.

5   Comandante Tacho expressed his gratitude and admiration for them when he said at the opening session of the National Democratic Convention: "These compañeros, these compañeras, these boys, these girls … it is they who kept the secret of our clandestine preparation … they took care of us when we were in the mountains of [the] Lacandon Jungle. They brought us tostadas, beans, *pinole*, and all

we needed"; see Comandante Insurgente Tacho, "CND: Apertura de la Plenaria: Bienvenidos a Bordo," Enlace Zapatista, August 3, 1994, accessed October 3, 2021, https://tinyurl.com/zhdwyxtc.

6   For an eloquent witness account of this meeting, see Lynn Stephen, "The Zapatista Army of National Liberation and the National Democratic Convention," *Latin American Perspectives* 22, no. 4 (Fall 1995): 88–99.

7   These two documents highlight the changes under Zapatismo in the lives of several Zapatista women, including Comandanta Ramona and Major Ana María; see Lourdes Consuelo Pacheco Ladrón de Guevara, "Nosotras ya Estábamos Muertas: Comandanta Ramona y Otras Insurgentas del Ejército Zapatista de Liberación Nacional"/"We Were Already Dead: Comandanta Ramona and Other Insurgents of the Zapatista Army of National Liberation," *Transcontinental Human Trajectories* 6 (2019), accessed October 4, 2021, https://www.unilim.fr/trahs/1881; Subcomandante Marcos, "12 Mujeres en el Año 12 (segundo de la guerra)," Enlace Zapatista, March 11, 1996, accessed October 4, 2021, https://enlacezapatista.ezln.org.mx/1996/03/11/12-mujeres-en-el-ano-12-segundo-de-la-guerra.

Not a Kids' Fable

1   See Dinah Livingstone, *Conversations with Durito: Stories of the Zapatistas and Neoliberalism* (Brooklyn, NY: Autonomedia, 2005), 118.

2   John Ross, *The War against Oblivion: Zapatista Chronicles 1994–2000* (Monroe, ME: Common Courage Press, 2000), 137–38.

Muting the Sound of War

1   See "A los Comités de Solidaridad con la Lucha Zapatista en Todo el Mundo," Enlace Zapatista, March 8, 1997, accessed November 10, 2021, https://tinyurl.com/2xrh4zh5.

2   See "421st Squadron, The Zapatista Maritime Delegation," April 20, 2021, Enlace Zapatista, accessed November 10, 2021, https://enlacezapatista.ezln.org.mx/2021/04/20/421st-squadron, as well as previous and subsequent communiqués.

3   In fact, they list those principled struggles in detail: against racism, patriarchy, religious intolerance, xenophobia, militarization, ecological destruction, fascism, segregation, moral hypocrisy, exclusion, war, hunger, the lack of housing, big capital, authoritarianism, dictatorship, the politics of economic liberalization, poverty, theft, corruption, discrimination, stupidity, lies, ignorance, slavery, injustice, oblivion, neoliberalism and for humanity.

A World Connected through Solidarity

1 Carlos Marín, "Plan del Ejército en Chiapas, desde 1994: Crear Bandas Paramilitares, Desplazar a la Población, Destruir las Bases de Apoyo del EZLN," *Semanario Proceso* no. 1105 (January 8,1998), accessed 11, 2021, http://historic.edualter.org/material/ddhh/proc1.htm; for an English translation, see "To Censure the Media, Control the Organizations of the Masses, Secretly Co-opt Civil Sectors....," accessed November 11, 2021, https://ratical.org/ratville/ArmyPlan94on.html.

2 For the resolution of the European Community, now the European Union, passed on February 2, 1998, really surprising in its detailed knowledge of events, see, Eur-Lex, accessed November 10, 2021, https://eur-lex.europa.eu/legal-content/EN/TXT/HTML/?uri=CELEX:51998IP0056&from=HU.

3 Changiz Varzi, "23 Years of Impunity for the Perpetrators of Acteal," *NACLA Reports,* December 22, 2020, accessed November 10, 2021, https://nacla.org/news/2020/12/21/23-years-impunity-acteal-massacre; for context, see Luis Hernández Navarro, "Noviembre en Aldama," *La Jornada,* November 24, 2020, accessed November 10, 2021, https://www.jornada.com.mx/2020/11/24/opinion/026a2pol.

4 Hermann Bellinghausen, "Chiapas: The Law of Déjà Vu," *La Jornada,* November 9, 2020, accessed November 10, 2021, https://chiapas-support.org/2020/09/21/chiapas-the-law-of-deja-vu.

5 The first in this series, "Part 6: A Mountain on the High Seas," was issued on October 5, 2020. Like the trip that intends to 'reverse' the voyage of the Conquest, the communiqués were issued in reverse order—until "Part 1: A Declaration...For Life" appeared on January 1, 2021. These and others that have followed in early 2021 are available at Enlace Zapatista, accessed November 10, 2021, https://enlacezapatista.ezln.org.mx.

6 See Raúl Romero, "El EZLN y la Otra Europa," *La Jornada*, January 2, 2021, accessed November 10, 2021, https://www.jornada.com.mx/notas/2021/01/02/politica/el-ezln-y-la-otra-europa.

An End to the War of Extermination

1 See Municipios Rebeldes Zapatistas y FZLN, *Fuerte Es Su Corazón* (Ediciones del Frente Zapatista de Liberación Nacional, 1998).

2 "Informe de los últimos resultados de nuestras investigaciones sobre la matanza de Acteal," Enlace Zapatista, December 26, 1997, accessed November 10, 2021, https://tinyurl.com/tahtjs2r.

3 Bishop Ruiz, following the Second Vatican Council in Rome in 1962, began a process of his own "conversion," first to the renovated church of Pope John XXIII, "the church of all, and especially the Church of the poor," and eventually to the church as imagined by the

Indigenous in his diocese. Following the Council of Latin American bishops in Medellin in 1968, which brought liberation theology to the region, the Catholic Church in Chiapas, under his leadership, was profoundly transformed—translating the Bible into Indigenous languages and forming over twenty thousand Indigenous catechists, who spread the radical message of equality and dignity for the poor. In 1974, ironically at the behest of the governor of Chiapas, Bishop Ruiz organized the first statewide Indigenous congress, which brought together all the indigenous catechists of Chiapas, many of whom later became insurgents in the EZLN. The congress is widely recognized as a turning point in indigenous organization in Chiapas. Bishop Ruiz was accepted as a trusted mediator by the Zapatistas in their peace talks with the government, heading the group called the Comisión Nacional de Intermediación (CONAI)—not to be confused with a subsequent group of mediators formed by members of the Mexican Congress, called the Comisión de Concordia y Pacificación (COCOPA); see John Womack, Jr., ed., *Rebellion in Chiapas: An Historical Reader* (New York: The New Press, 1999).

4   See "Communiqué from San Pedro Chenalhó, autonomous municipality in Los Altos, February 16, 1998," in Municipios Rebeldes Zapatistas y FZLN, *Fuerte Es Su Corazón* (Ediciones del Frente Zapatista de Liberación Nacional, 1998). "The government has gotten it into its head to destroy the installations of the autonomous municipal capitals with the pretext of defending the rule of law, jailing the authorities and some inhabitants of the autonomous municipalities, accusing them of stealing and usurping authority." Then they ask, "Who is the real usurper who owes his position to the assassination perpetrated by his own political party?" The writers know that Mexicans will guess their answer: it's Zedillo, who became president by usurping the position following the murder of Colosio. He is the usurper, or at least that's what they claim, turning the accusation around to remind the president of how he got to power.

5   It is estimated that by the end of 1997 eleven thousand people were displaced from their homes and villages, turned into refugees as a result of paramilitary activity; see Víctor Mariña, Mario Viveros, Nancy Ventura, Carlos Mendoza, Bernardo Ezeta, Jenaro Villamil, and Martha Zepeda, *Zapatistas: Crónica de una Rebelión* (video; English subtitles), YouTube, accessed November 10, 2021, https://www.youtube.com/watch?v=D6j7e1uK5cQ.

6   This municipality is named after the anarchist thinker and organizer who preceded and helped to impel the Mexican Revolution.

7   Valdez Ruvalcaba also stresses the surprising method of collective, anonymous work in which all the members of the community felt that this was their work, even if they had not participated in the

painting; they arrived and said, "'see how beautiful my mural looks' ... they claimed it as their own"; Jeff Conant, "Life and Dreams of the Perla River Valley: A River That Runs through History: Interview with Sergio Valdez Ruvalcaba," Watering Hole: Jeff Conant (blog), March 2, 2013, accessed November 11, 2021, https://tinyurl.com/ht587z4x.

8   Amnistía Internacional, "El Mural Mágico de Taniperla," 2008, accessed November 10, 2021, http://www.amnistiacatalunya.org/edu/3/txt-taniperla.html.

9   On the significance of the milpa, see Armando Bartra, "De Milpas, Mujeres y Otros Mitotes," *La Jornada del Campo* no. 31, April 17, 2010, accessed November 10, 2021, https://www.jornada.com.mx/2010/04/17/milpas.html; he writes, *"Los mesoamericanos no sembramos maíz, los mesoamericanos hacemos milpa. Y son cosas distintas porque el maíz es una planta y la milpa, un modo de vida"* [We Mesoamericans don't grow corn, we make a milpa. These are different: corn is a plant, the milpa is a way of life].

10 This communiqué was issued on May 25, 1998, by the Zapatista bases of support and the ARIC-Independiente of Taniperla.

A Matter of Time

1   Chavajeval and Unión Progreso, mentioned by the Sup in the communiqué published on the same date as this story, were the sites of deadly attacks on the previous day—by the army and state and federal police forces, not paramilitaries; see Hermann Bellinghausen, "Exigen en Chiapas Cese el Acoso Judicial contra Comunidades," *La Jornada*, June 11, 2012, accessed November 10, 2021, https://www.jornada.com.mx/2012/06/11/politica/022n1pol, while fourteen years after the massacre near El Bosque, the communities were still protesting that no one had ever been charged in "one of the least investigated state crimes in recent history."

On Autonomous Education

1   See the next story in our collection, "We Who Came After Did Understand," read by Marcos at the meeting of August 31, 1999.

2   Prior to the rebellion, only about a third of the children in Chiapas completed primary school, the overwhelming majority of those being boys; see Neil Harvey, *The Chiapas Rebellion: The Struggle for Land and Democracy* (Durham, NC: Duke University Press, 1998), 184.

3   It is significant that the Zapatistas' "Little School" of 2012–2013, an invitation to supporters to come to Chiapas to learn from their ten years' experience of autonomy, did not take place in classrooms but in the communities, where students lived with the Zapatista families who were their teachers. Mariana Mora emphasizes that the main

lesson of the *Escuelita* "was that knowledge production emerges not by extracting the student from daily life into a classroom but as the body moves through and acts within daily life … in the cornfield, in the mountains, the small conversations over coffee in the kitchen while breakfast is being made, that's where learning takes place"; Mariana Mora, *Kuxlejal Politics: Indigenous Autonomy, Race, and Decolonizing Research in Zapatista Communities* (Austin: University of Texas Press, 2017), 236.

4   See Subcomandante Insurgente Moisés, "Communique from the EZLN's CCRI-CG: And We Broke the Siege," Enlace Zapatista, August 20, 2019, accessed November 11, 2021, tinyurl.com/24ncxktme.

5   W.E.B. Du Bois, *The Souls of Black Folk* (1903), Project Gutenberg, accessed November 11, 2021, https://www.gutenberg.org/files/408/408-h/408-h.htm; in chapter one, "Of our Spiritual Striving," Du Bois defines double consciousness as "this sense of always looking at one's self through the eyes of others, of measuring one's soul by the tape of a world that looks on in amused contempt and pity"; Frantz Fanon, *Black Skin, White Masks* (London: Pluto Press, 1986 [1952]), 111–12.

The Zapatista Legacy

1   The 1917 Constitution created the ejidos by expropriating hacienda lands. For the significance of the 1992 neoliberal reform, which brought an end to land redistribution, see our commentary on "Story of Durito": "Durito and Zapata Do Remember," pages 45–47.

2   In 1936, the Sindicato Mexicano de Electricistas (SME) went on strike against the US, British, and Canadian owners of the electrical company Luz y Fuerza. Mexico City had no electricity for ninety days. However, the strike was successful and led to the negotiation of one of the most important labor contracts in Latin America. This contract preserved SME's independence from the government, unlike the case of other Mexican unions; see Massimo Modenesi, Lucio Oliver, Mariana López de la Vega, and Fernando Munguía Galean, "La Lucha del Sindicato Mexicano de Electricistas," *OSAL* 11, no. 27 (April 2010), accessed November 11, 2021, http://biblioteca.clacso.edu.ar/ar/libros/osal/osal27/11Modonesi.pdf.

3   Julia Preston, "Student Strike in Capital Jarring All of Mexico," *New York Times*, June 25, 1999, accessed November 11, 2021, https://tinyurl.com/ywpxchsy.

4   "Chiapas: la Guerra. III. Amador Hernández, la Disputa por la Tierra (Carta 5.3)," Enlace Zapatista, November 20, 1999, accessed November 11, 2021, https://tinyurl.com/4wwf65p4.

5   The Sup frequently alludes to August as the month of memory and beautiful dawns; see footnote, page 29.

6   Subcomandante Marcos, "17 de Noviembre de 2006, 23 Años de EZLN," Enlace Zapatista, November 18, 2006, accessed November 11, 2021, http://enlacezapatista.ezln.org.mx/2006/11/18/17-de-noviembre-de-2006-23-anos.

7   From 2003 on, the Zapatistas designated their autonomous regions "caracoles"—literally referencing the conch shell used to convoke communal assemblies in pre-Columbian times; see Subcomandante Marcos, "Coloquio Aubry. Parte VII. (y última) Sentir el Rojo," December 17, 2007, accessed November 11, 2021, https://tinyurl.com/nrpfddwr; for further elaboration of the multiple meanings of the caracol, see, Subcomandante Insurgente Marcos, "Chiapas: The Thirteenth Stele" (excerpts), July 21, 2003, accessed November 11, 2021, https://www.schoolsforchiapas.org/wp-content/uploads/2014/03/13th-Stele-Excerpts.pdf.

8   "Autogobierno y autonomía de las comunidades zapatistas," Zapateando, January 2, 2014, accessed November 11, 2021, https://tinyurl.com/4c2hsdxh.

9   For an account of this surprising development, see "We Broke the Siege", Enlace Zapatista, August 17, 2019, accessed November 11, 2021, http://enlacezapatista.ezln.org.mx/2019/08/20/communique-from-the-ezlns-ccri-cg-and-we-broke-the-siege.

10 The house has been renamed Casa de Todas y Todos and works on the recovery of Mexican historical memory and the investigation of state repression and the search for its victims; see "El comandante Germán presenta la Casa de Todos y Todas, centrada la búsqueda de las víctimas," Noticias de Navarra, May 2, 2014, accessed November 11, 2021, https://tinyurl.com/hw98wskd.

11 Marcos, "17 de Noviembre de 2006."

Some Room Left for Love and Poetry

1   Subcomandante Marcos, "Heroísmo Cotidiano Hace Posible Que Existan Los Destellos," Enlace Zapatista, January 26, 1994, accessed November 11, 2021, https://tinyurl.com/5uzzx4p4.

2   See Melissa Forbis, "Hacia la Autonomía: Zapatista Women Developing a New World," in Christine Eber and Christine Kovic, eds., Women of Chiapas: Making History in Times of Struggle and Hope (New York: Routledge, 2003).

3   While it is hard not to wince at what appears to be a naturalization of gender and the heterosexual couple, this letter precedes the Zapatistas' direct contact with "other loves" (LGBTQ people), whose solidarities and struggles they engaged during the Other Campaign of 2006. Such apparently unconscious heteronormative assumptions no longer appear in Zapatista discourse, as far as we have been able to discover. Occasionally, even earlier, one finds

recognition of sexual diversity: "*Los y las zapatistas y quienes no son ni los ni las, pero son zapatistas, saludamos la dignidad lésbica, gay, transgenérica y bisexual.*" [Zapatista men and women and those who are neither men nor women but Zapatistas salute the dignity of the lesbian, gay, transgender, and bisexual communities]. "Saludo a la 21 Marcha del orgullo lésbico, gay, transgenérico y bisexual," Enlace Zapatista, June 27, 1999, accessed November 11, 2021, https://tinyurl.com/4jkjxsr4; also see "The Tale of the Pink Shoelaces," in *Our Word Is Our* Weapon, trans. Juana Ponce de León, (New York: Penguin 2002), 76, accessed November 11, https://theanarchistlibrary.org/library/subcomandante-marcos-our-word-is-our-weapon.

Afterword

1   "421st Squadron," Enlace Zapatista, April 2021, accessed March 18, 2022, https://enlacezapatista.ezln.org.mx/2021/04/20/421st-squadron.

2   *Extemporánea* means *out of synch* or *untimely*, a term the Zapatistas embraced as a descriptor for their journey. They chose this name for their delegation because *Extemporánea* was the word stamped on their passports when they finally secured them, having suffered innumerable bureaucratic delays due to incomplete documentation of their very existence (birth certificates registered with the state, etc.).

3   Marijose can be seen making this pronouncement in "The Landing," Enlace Zapatista, June 30, 2021, accessed March 18, 2022, https://enlacezapatista.ezln.org.mx/2021/06/30/the-landing.

4   For the transcribed speeches of each of the members of the Zapatista maritime squadron and a video with the float rolling through the streets of Madrid, see "Only 500 Years Later," August 13, 2021, accessed March 18, 2022, https://enlacezapatista.ezln.org.mx/2021/08/17/only-500-years-later.

5   Oleg Yasinsky, "Antes de que Putin Nos Invada," Pressenza, December 11, 2021, accessed March 18, 2022, https://www.pressenza.com/es/2021/12/antes-de-que-putin-nos-invada; Yasinsky, the first translator of Zapatista texts into Russian, recorded a video interview with Subcomandante Moisés, which is included in the commentary by the Russian artistic collective Chto Delat, "Slow Orientation in Zapatism," 2017, accessed March 18, 2022, https://tinyurl.com/5ajpcjm2.

6   Brenda Norrell, "Sami in Far North Welcome Zapatistas on 'Journey for Life,'" Censored News, September 25, 2021, accessed March 21, 2022, https://bsnorrell.blogspot.com/2021/09/sami-in-far-north-finland-welcome.html.

7   "The Misnamed 'Mayan Train': Multimodal Land Grabbing," Grain, March 3, 2020, accessed March 21, 2022, https://grain.org/en/article/6423-the-misnamed-mayan-train-multimodal-land-grabbing.

8   Tom Wall, "The Battle to Save Lapland: 'First, They Took the Religion. Now They Want to Build a Railroad,'" *Guardian*, February 23, 2019, accessed March 21, 2022, https://www.theguardian.com/world/2019/feb/23/battle-save-lapland-want-to-build-railroad; a slightly later publication gives both opposing views and is definitely worth reading: Eilís Quinn, "The Arctic Railway: Building a Future or Destroying a Culture?" Rail-Bus, accessed March 21, 2022, https://railbus.com.ng/index.php/firms/the-arctic-railway-building-a-future-or-destroying-a-culture.

9   Kim Willsher, "End of la ZAD? France's 'Utopian' Anti-Airport Community Faces Bitter Last Stand," *Guardian*, December 28, 2017, accessed March 21, 2022, https://www.theguardian.com/profile/kim-willsher; "The Revenge against the Commons," ZAD Forever, April 24, 2018, accessed March 21, 2022, https://zadforever.blog/2018/04/24/the-revenge-against-the-commons.

10 For an informative report on this and other European encounters, see Aída Hernández Castillo, "Building Alliances in Pandemic Times: The Zapatista Journey through Europe," International Work Group for Indigenous Affairs (IWGIA), August 30, 2021, accessed March 21, 2022, https://tinyurl.com/5n9a3w8p.

11 Daliri Oropeza, "Zapatistas, Women, and Gender Dissidents: On the Encounter in Notre Dame des Landes," Pié de Página, August 18, 2021, accessed March 21, 2022, https://tinyurl.com/4ynsxsf3.

12 Petar Stanchev, "From Chiapas to Rojava: Seas Divide Us, Autonomy Binds Us," *Roar*, February 17, 2015, accessed March 21, 2022, https://roarmag.org/essays/chiapas-rojava-zapatista-kurds.

13 Charlotte María Sáenz, "Women Up in Arms: Zapatistas and Rojava Kurds Embrace a New Gender Politics," Truthout, March 19, 2015, accessed March 21, 2022, https://tinyurl.com/3m2dzh5u.

14 Muireann de Barra, dir., *Muralistas*, Gaffer Productions, 2000, accessed March 21, 2022, https://youtu.be/b8HMyUSLGDY; filmed in Dublin, Ireland, and Chiapas, Mexico, in 1999, with the participation of SAOL project.

15 Al Faro Zapatista, accessed March 21, 2022, http://alfarozapatista.jkopkutik.org.

16 La Hora de los Pequeños. Durito, Carta 4a," Enlace Zapatista, October 13, 1999, accessed March 21, 2022, https://enlacezapatista.ezln.org.mx/1999/10/13/la-hora-de-los-pequenos-durito-carta-4a.

Bibliography

Bacon, David. "The Rebirth of Mexico's Electrical Workers." *NACLA Report*, February 7, 2019. Accessed November 11, 2021. https://nacla.org/news/2019/02/07/rebirth-mexico's-electrical-workers.

Bartra, Armando. "De Milpas, Mujeres y Otros Mitotes." *La Jornada del Campo* no. 31, April 17, 2010. Accessed November 10, 2021. https://www.jornada.com.mx/2010/04/17/milpas.html.

Bellinghausen, Hermann. "Chiapas: The Law of Déjà Vu." Chiapas Support Committee, September 21, 2020. Accessed November 9, 2021. https://chiapas-support.org/2020/09/21/chiapas-the-law-of-deja-vu.

———. "Exigen en Chiapas Cese Acoso Judicial contra Comunidades." *La Jornada,* June 11, 2012. Accessed November 11, 2021. https://www.jornada.com.mx/2012/06/11/politica/022n1pol.

Briy, Anya. "Zapatistas at 26: Autonomy and Women's Liberation," March 31, 2020. Accessed October 3, 2021. https://tinyurl.com/2uke3ruw.

Brus Li, Comandante. "Palabras para los Pueblos Indígenas." Enlace Zapatista, January 1, 2003. Accessed October 3, 2021. https://tinyurl.com/ahw9dr3j.

Caballero, Luci, and Verónica Gago. "The Political Invention of the Feminist Strike." *Viewpoint Magazine*, March 23, 2021. Accessed October 3, 2021. https://viewpointmag.com/2021/03/23/the-political-invention-of-the-feminist-strike.

CCRI-CG. "Al Pueblo de México: el Diálogo de San Cristóbal Fue Verdadero." Enlace Zapatista, March 1, 1994. Accessed November 11, 2021. https://tinyurl.com/25jm9yf5.

———. "Al pueblo de México: en Nuestros Sueños Hemos Visto Otro Mundo." Enlace Zapatista, March 1, 1994. Accessed November 11, 2021. https://tinyurl.com/45jydajr.

Cerullo, Margaret. "The Zapatistas' Other Politics: The Subjects of Autonomy." In *Engaging Social Justice: Critical Studies of 21st Century Social Transformation*. Edited by David Fasenfest, 289–99. Leiden, NL: Brill, 2009.

Conant, Jeff. "Life and Dreams of the Perla River Valley: A River That Runs through History: Interview with Sergio Valdez Ruvalcaba." The Watering Hole: Jeff Conant (blog), March 2, 2013. Accessed November 11, 2021. https://tinyurl.com/ht587z4x.

Cortés, Alberto, dir. *Corazon del Tiempo*. Mexico: IMCINE/Filomteca UNAM, 2009.

Darío, Rubén. "To Roosevelt." 1904. Accessed October 3, 2021. https://tinyurl.com/533wbbt7.

Défossé, Nicolás. *¡Viva Mexico!* Chiapas, MX: Terra Nostra Films, 2010. Accessed October 3, 2021. https://centroprodh.org.mx/sididh_2_0_alfa/?p=30799.

del Castillo Troncoso, Alberto. *Las Mujeres de X'oyep: La Historia detrás de la Fotografía*. México: CONACULTA/Cenart/Centro de la Imagen, 2013.

DuBois, W.E.B. "Of Our Spiritual Strivings." In *The Souls of Black Folk* (1903). Project Gutenberg. Accessed November 11, 2021. https://www.gutenberg.org/files/408/408-h/408-h.htm.

Enlace Zapatista. EZLN Documents (1993–2021). Accessed September 28, 2021. http://enlacezapatista.ezln.org.mx/category/comunicado.

"Escuelita Textbooks." Accessed November 11, 2021. https://escuelitabooks.blogspot.com/2014/06/all-books-are-available.html.

Faith, S. "Suffrage, Liberation and Checking Your Engine." Blog of Toledo Lucas County Public Library. Unavailable November 11, 2021. https://www.toledolibrary.org/blog/suffrage-liberation-and-checking-your-engine.

Fanon, Frantz. *Black Skin, White Masks*. London: Pluto Press, 1986 [1952].

Fernández Christlieb, Paulina. *Justicia Autónoma Zapatista. Zona Selva Tzeltal*. México: Estampa/Ediciones Autónom@s, 2014.

Fitzwater, Dylan. *Autonomy Is in Our Hearts: Zapatista Autonomous Government through the Lens of the Tsotsil Language*. Oakland: PM Press, 2019.

Forbis, Melissa. "Hacia la Autonomía: Zapatista Women Developing a New World." In *Women of Chiapas: Making History in Times of Struggle and Hope*. Edited by Christine Eber and Christine Kovic, ch. 22. New York: Routledge, 2003.

———. "'Never Again a Mexico without Us:' Gender, Indigenous Autonomy, and Multiculturalism in Neoliberal Mexico." PhD diss., University of Texas, 2008. Accessed October 3, 2021. https://repositories.lib.utexas.edu/handle/2152/18324.

Freidel, David, Linda Schele, and Joy Parker. *Maya Cosmos: Three Thousand Years on the Shaman's Path*. New York: William Morrow, 1993.

Galeano, Subcomandante Insurgente. "421st Squadron, the Zapatista Maritime Delegation." Enlace Zapatista, April 17, 2021. Accessed September 28, 2021. http://enlacezapatista.ezln.org.mx/2021/04/17/escuadron-421.

———. "From the Notebook of the Cat-Dog: Preparations for the Puy Ta Cuxlejaltic Film Festival, a CompArte Focused on Dance, and the Second International Gathering for Women Who Struggle." Enlace Zapatista, September 16, 2019. Accessed September 28, 2021. https://tinyurl.com/u7366da.

Gibler, John. *I Couldn't Even Imagine They Would Kill Us: An Oral History of the Attacks against the Students of Ayotzinapa*. Foreword Ariel Dorfman. Open Media Series. San Francisco: City Lights Books, 2017.

Harvey, David. *A Brief History of Neoliberalism*. New York: Oxford University Press, 2007.

———. "The Neoliberal Project Is Alive but Has Lost Its Legitimacy." Wire, February 9, 2019. Accessed October 3, 2021. https://thewire.in/economy/david-harvey-marxist-scholar-neo-liberalism.

Harvey, Neil. *The Chiapas Rebellion: The Struggle for Land and Democracy*. Durham, NC: Duke University Press, 1998.

Hernández Navarro, Luis. "Noviembre en Aldama." *La Jornada*, November 24, 2020. Accessed November 10, 2021. https://www.jornada.com.mx/2020/11/24/opinion/026a2pol.

Higgins, Nicholas. *Understanding the Chiapas Rebellion: Modernist Visions and the Invisible Indian*. Austin: University of Texas Press, 2004.

Irurzun, Patxi. "El Mural Mágico de Taniperla." Amnistía Internacional, 2008. Accessed November 10, 2021. http://www.amnistiacatalunya.org/edu/3/txt-taniperla.html.

Elaine Katzenberger, ed., *First World, Ha Ha Ha! The Zapatista Challenge*. San Francisco: City Lights, 1995.

Kelly, James J. "Article 27 and Mexican Land Reform: The Legacy of Zapata's Dream," *Columbia Human Rights Law Review* 25 (1993–1994): 541–70.

Keppler, Emily. "Another Government Is Possible." Intercontinental Cry, October 17, 2016. Accessed October 3, 2021. https://intercontinentalcry.org/another-government-possible.

Klein, Hillary. *Compañeras: Zapatista Women's Stories*. New York: Seven Stories Press, 2015.

Kopkind, Andrew. "Opening Shot" (editorial). *Nation* 258, no. 4 (January 31, 1994); Reprinted in *The Zapatista Reader*. Edited by Tom Hayden, 19–20. New York: Thunder's Mouth Press/Nation Books, 2002.

Lenkersdorf, Carlos. *Los Hombres Verdaderos: Voces y Testimonios Tojolabales*. México D.F., Madrid: Siglo XXI, 1996.

Lomnitz, Claudio. "The Maya Train: The Zapatistas Are Right." Chiapas Support Committee, January 20, 2019. Accessed September 28, 2021. https://chiapas-support.org/2019/01/20/the-maya-train-the-zapatistas-are-right.

Mallon, Florencia. "Indigenous Peoples and Nation States in Spanish America, 1780–2000." *The Oxford Handbook of Latin American History*. Edited by José C. Moya. New York: Oxford University Press, 2010.

Marcos, Subcomandante Insurgente. "A Los Comités de Solidaridad con la Lucha Zapatista en Todo el Mundo: Anuncio de Nuevo Encuentro de Rebeldías y Resistencias." Enlace Zapatista, March 8, 1997. Accessed November 10, 2021. https://tinyurl.com/2xrh4zh5.

———. "Chiapas: la Guerra. III. Amador Hernández, la Disputa por la Tierra. Carta 5.3." Enlace Zapatista, November 20, 1999. Accessed November 11, 2021. https://tinyurl.com/53tdrr9d.

———. "Chiapas: The Thirteenth Stele" (excerpts). *Schools for Chiapas*, July 2003. Accessed November 11, 2021. https://tinyurl.com/nrpfddwr.

———. "Coloquio Aubry. Parte VII. (y última) 'Sentir el Rojo.'" Enlace Zapatista, December 17, 2007. Accessed November 11, 2021. https://tinyurl.com/nrpfddwr.

———. *Conversations with Durito: Stories of the Zapatistas and Neoliberalism*. Edited and introduced by Acción Zapatista Editorial Collective. Brooklyn, NY: Autonomedia, 2005.

———. "The Fourth World War Has Begun." *Le Monde Diplomatique*, September 1997. Accessed October 3, 2021. https://mondediplo.com/1997/09/marcos.

———. "Heroísmo Cotidiano Hace Posible Que Existan los Destellos." Enlace Zapatista, January 26, 1994. Accessed November 11, 2021. https://tinyurl.com/5uzzx4p4.

———. "Historia de las Preguntas." Enlace Zapatista, December 13, 1994. Accessed November 11, 2021. http://enlacezapatista.ezln.org.mx/1994/12/13/la-historia-de-las-preguntas. Published in a bilingual Spanish-English edition in Subcomandante Marcos, *Questions and Swords: Folktales of the Zapatista Revolution*. El Paso, TX: Cinco Puntos Press, 2001.

———. "Informe de los últimos resultados de nuestras investigaciones sobre la matanza de Acteal." Enlace Zapatista, December 26, 1997. Accessed November 10, 2021. https://tinyurl.com/tahtjs2r.

———. *Los Otros Cuentos*. Buenos Aires, AR: Red de Solidaridad con Chiapas, 2008.

———. "Saludo a la 21 marcha del orgullo lésbico, gay, transgenérico y bisexual." Enlace Zapatista, June 27, 1999. Accessed November 11, 2021. https://tinyurl.com/4jkjxsr4.

———. "17 de Noviembre de 2006: 23 Años del EZLN." Enlace Zapatista, November 18, 2006. Accessed September 28, 2021. https://enlacezapatista.ezln.org.mx/2006/11/18/17-de-noviembre-de-2006-23-anos.

———. "Sobre el Asesinato de Colosio: Ellos … ¿Por Qué…?" Enlace Zapatista, March 24, 1994. Accessed October 3, 2021. https://tinyurl.com/rt3v2fz7.

———. "The Tale of the Pink Shoelaces." In *Our Word Is Our Weapon*. Trans. Juana Ponce de León. New York: Seven Stories Press, 2001. Accessed November 11, 2021. https://theanarchistlibrary.org/library/subcommandante-marcos-our-word-is-our-weapon.

———. "12 Mujeres en el Año 12 (segundo de la guerra)." Enlace Zapatista, March 11, 1996. Accessed October 4, 2021. https://enlacezapatista.ezln.org.mx/1996/03/11/12-mujeres-en-el-ano-12-segundo-de-la-guerra.

Marijose. *Arrival in Vigo, Portugal* (video). Accessed September 28, 2021. https://vimeo.com/566701998.

Marín, Carlos. "Plan del Ejército en Chiapas, desde 1994: Crear Bandas Paramilitares, Desplazar a la Población, Destruir las Bases de Apoyo del EZLN…" *Semanario Proceso* no. 1105 (January 4, 1998). Accessed November 11, 2021. http://historic.edualter.org/material/ddhh/proc1.htm. For an English translation, see "To Censure the Media, Control the Organizations of the Masses, Secretly Co-opt Civil Sectors…" Accessed November 11, 2021. https://ratical.org/ratville/ArmyPlan94on.html.

Mariña, Víctor, Mario Viveros, Nancy Ventura, Carlos Mendoza, Bernardo Ezeta, Jenaro Villamil, and Martha Zepeda. *Zapatistas: Crónica de una Rebelión* (video; English subtitles). YouTube. Accessed November 10, 2021. https://youtu.be/D6j7e1uK5cQ.

Modenesi, Massimo, Lucio Oliver, Mariana López de la Vega, and Fernando Munguía Galean. "La lucha del Sindicato Mexicano de Electricistas." *OSAL*, 11, no. 27 (April 2010). Accessed November 11, 2021. http://biblioteca.clacso.edu.ar/ar/libros/osal/osal27/11Modonesi.pdf.

Moisés, Subcomandante Insurgente. "Communique from the EZLN's CCRI-CG: And We Broke the Siege." Enlace Zapatista, August 20, 2019. Accessed November 11, 2021. tinyurl.com/24ncxktm.

———. "For Life: The Departure of 'La Extemporánea' to Europe." Enlace Zapatista, September 3, 2021. Accessed November 11, 2021. https://tinyurl.com/58wwaht8.

Mora, Mariana. *Kuxlejal Politics: Indigenous Autonomy, Race and Decolonizing Research in Zapatista Communities*. Austin: University of Texas Press, 2017.

Municipios Rebeldes Zapatistas y FZLN. *Fuerte Es Su Corazón*. México: Ediciones del Frente Zapatista de Liberación Nacional, 1998.

Pacheco Ladrón de Guevara, Lourdes Consuelo. "Nosotras Ya Estábamos Muertas: Comandanta Ramona y Otras Insurgentas del Ejército Zapatista de Liberación Nacional"/"We Were Already Dead: Comandanta Ramona and Other Insurgents of the Zapatista Army of National Liberation." *Transcontinental Human Trajectories* no. 6 (2019). Accessed October 4, 2021. https://www.unilim.fr/trahs/1881.

Preston, Julia. "Student Strike in Capital Jarring All of Mexico." *New York Times*, June 25, 1999. Accessed November 11, 2021. https://tinyurl.com/ywpxchsy.

Romero, Raúl. "El EZLN y la Otra Europa." *La Jornada*, January 2, 2021. Accessed November 10, 2021. https://www.jornada.com.mx/notas/2021/01/02/politica/el-ezln-y-la-otra-europa.

Ross, John. *The War against Oblivion: Zapatista Chronicles 1994–2000*. Monroe, ME: Common Courage Press, 2000.

Salazar, Miguel. "The Problem with Latinidad." *Nation*, September 16, 2019. Accessed September 28, 2021. https://www.thenation.com/article/archive/hispanic-heritage-month-latinidad.

Stephen, Lynn. "The Zapatista Army of National Liberation and the National Democratic Convention." *Latin American Perspectives* 22, no. 4 (Fall 1995): 88–99.

Tacho, Comandante Insurgente. "CND: Apertura de la Plenaria: Bienvenidos a Bordo." Enlace Zapatista, August 3, 1994. Accessed October 3, 2021. https://tinyurl.com/zhdwyxtc.

———. "Siete Mensajes durante la Ceremonia de Entrega del Bastón de Mando al Subcomandante Marcos." Enlace Zapatista, November 17, 1994. Accessed October 3, 2021. https://tinyurl.com/2hmupt8n.

Varzi, Changiz M. "23 Years of Impunity for the Perpetrators of Acteal." *NACLA Reports*, December 22, 2020. Accessed November 10, 2021. https://nacla.org/news/2020/12/21/23-years-impunity-acteal-massacre.

Villoro, Juan. "Prohibido Votar por una Indígena." *New York Times* (Spanish edition), February 24, 2018. Accessed September 28, 2021. https://www.nytimes.com/es/2018/02/24/espanol/opinion/opinion-villoro-marichuy.html.

Vos, Jan de. *Una Tierra para Sembrar Sueños: Historia Reciente de la Selva Lacandona, 1950-2000*. México: CIESAS, Fondo de Cultura Económica, 2002.

———. *Vienen de Lejos los Torrentes: una Historia de Chiapas*. Tuxtla Gutiérrez, Chiapas, México: Consejo Estatal para las Culturas y las Artes de Chiapas, 2010.

Womack, John, Jr., ed. *Rebellion in Chiapas: An Historical Reader*. New York: New Press, 1999.

Zapatista Army of National Liberation. "Letter from the Zapatista Women to Women in Struggle Around the World." Enlace Zapatista, February 13, 2019. Accessed September 28, 2021. https://tinyurl.com/rm96km2w.

———. "We Don't Need Permission to Fight for Life: Zapatista Women Join the March 9 National Strike." Enlace Zapatista, March 5, 2020. Accessed October 3, 2021. https://tinyurl.com/uxfznp6e.

"Zapatistas Silent Mobilization (December 21, 2012)." Dorset Chiapas Solidarity, December 25, 2012. Accessed October 3, 2021. https://dorsetchiapassolidarity.wordpress.com/2012/12/25/zapatistas-silent-mobilization-december-21-2012.

Zibechi, Raúl. "The Schools from Below." *In Motion Magazine*, September 15, 2013. Accessed September 28, 2021. https://inmotionmagazine.com/global/r_zibechi_escuelitas.html. Originally published in *La Jornada*, August 23, 2013.

About the Contributors

Subcomandante Marcos is the military commander and longtime spokesperson of the Zapatista Army of National Liberation (EZLN). "Marcos" disappeared from the stage in May 2014, when the Zapatistas decided his role as their main spokesperson had come to an end. He was reborn as Galeano, the *nombre de lucha* of a Zapatista schoolteacher murdered that month by paramilitaries. He has continued to issue stories and communiqués, the latter often co-authored with Subcomandante Moisés.

JoAnn Wypijewski is an independent writer, editor, and journalist based in New York. Her work has appeared in numerous magazines, including *Mother Jones* and the *Nation*. She is the author of *What We Don't Talk About: Sex and the Mess of Life*.

Antonia Carcelén-Estrada is a translator and activist for the revitalization of Indigenous languages and environmental rights. She has taught at Universidad San Francisco de Quito since 2018. Her academic interests include colonial and post-colonial Abya-Yala and transatlantic dialogues on political philosophy, cultural studies, and orality.

Margaret Cerullo has been following the Zapatistas avidly since she found herself in Mexico for the first time in January

1994. She is a member of the East Coast Chiapas Solidarity Committee, which certifies students to attend the Zapatista language school in Oventic. She teaches at Hampshire College.

Marina Kaplan is emeritus professor of Spanish and Latin American Studies at Smith College. She has visited Zapatista autonomous communities three times throughout the years. She is interested in the tension between modern alienation and postmodern movements often evoked in the reading of Marcos.

Zack Zucker attended the Escuelita in 2012 and shared his notebooks, but, most importantly, he has a gifted sense for language that saved us in many hard places of translation. He is a nurse in Greenfield, Massachusetts, and the proud father of Ramona, our little *comandanta*.

ABOUT PM PRESS

PM Press is an independent, radical publisher of books and media to educate, entertain, and inspire. Founded in 2007 by a small group of people with decades of publishing, media, and organizing experience, PM Press amplifies the voices of radical authors, artists, and activists. Our aim is to deliver bold political ideas and vital stories to all walks of life and arm the dreamers to demand the impossible. We have sold millions of copies of our books, most often one at a time, face to face. We're old enough to know what we're doing and young enough to know what's at stake. Join us to create a better world.

PM Press
PO Box 23912
Oakland, CA 94623
www.pmpress.org

PM Press in Europe
europe@pmpress.org
www.pmpress.org.uk

FRIENDS OF PM PRESS

These are indisputably momentous times—the financial system is melting down globally and the Empire is stumbling. Now more than ever there is a vital need for radical ideas.

In the many years since its founding—and on a mere shoestring—PM Press has risen to the formidable challenge of publishing and distributing knowledge and entertainment for the struggles ahead. With hundreds of releases to date, we have published an impressive and stimulating array of literature, art, music, politics, and culture. Using every available medium, we've succeeded in connecting those hungry for ideas and information to those putting them into practice.

Friends of PM allows you to directly help impact, amplify, and revitalize the discourse and actions of radical writers, filmmakers, and artists. It provides us with a stable foundation from which we can build upon our early successes and provides a much-needed subsidy for the materials that can't necessarily pay their own way. You can help make that happen—and receive every new title automatically delivered to your door once a month—by joining as a Friend of PM Press. And, we'll throw in a free T-shirt when you sign up.

Here are your options:

- **$30 a month** Get all books and pamphlets plus 50% discount on all webstore purchases

- **$40 a month** Get all PM Press releases (including CDs and DVDs) plus 50% discount on all webstore purchases

- **$100 a month** Superstar—Everything plus PM merchandise, free downloads, and 50% discount on all webstore purchases

For those who can't afford $30 or more a month, we have **Sustainer Rates** at $15, $10 and $5. Sustainers get a free PM Press T-shirt and a 50% discount on all purchases from our website.

Your Visa or Mastercard will be billed once a month, until you tell us to stop. Or until our efforts succeed in bringing the revolution around. Or the financial meltdown of Capital makes plastic redundant. Whichever comes first.

DEPARTMENT OF ANTHROPOLOGY & SOCIAL CHANGE

Anthropology and Social Change, housed within the California Institute of Integral Studies, is a small innovative graduate department with a particular focus on activist scholarship, militant research, and social change. We offer both masters and doctoral degree programs.

Our unique approach to collaborative research methodology dissolves traditional barriers between research and political activism, between insiders and outsiders, and between researchers and protagonists. Activist research is a tool for "creating the conditions we describe." We engage in the process of co-research to explore existing alternatives and possibilities for social change.

Anthropology and Social Change
anth@ciis.edu
1453 Mission Street
94103
San Francisco, California
www.ciis.edu/academics/graduate-programs/anthropology-and-social-change

Autonomy Is in Our Hearts: Zapatista Autonomous Government through the Lens of the Tsotsil Language

Dylan Eldredge Fitzwater
with a Foreword by John P. Clark

ISBN: 978-1-62963-580-4
$19.95   224 pages

Following the Zapatista uprising on New Year's Day 1994, the EZLN communities of Chiapas began the slow process of creating a system of autonomous government that would bring their call for freedom, justice, and democracy from word to reality. *Autonomy Is in Our Hearts* analyzes this long and arduous process on its own terms, using the conceptual language of Tsotsil, a Mayan language indigenous to the highland Zapatista communities of Chiapas.

The words "Freedom," "Justice," and "Democracy" emblazoned on the Zapatista flags are only approximations of the aspirations articulated in the six indigenous languages spoken by the Zapatista communities. They are rough translations of concepts such as *ichbail ta muk'* or "mutual recognition and respect among equal persons or peoples," *a'mtel* or "collective work done for the good of a community" and *lekil kuxlejal* or "the life that is good for everyone." *Autonomy Is in Our Hearts* provides a fresh perspective on the Zapatistas and a deep engagement with the daily realities of Zapatista autonomous government. Simultaneously an exposition of Tsotsil philosophy and a detailed account of Zapatista governance structures, this book is an indispensable commentary on the Zapatista movement of today.

"This is a refreshing book. Written with the humility of the learner, or the absence of the arrogant knower, the Zapatista dictum to 'command obeying' becomes to 'know learning.'"
—Marisol de la Cadena, author of *Earth Beings: Ecologies of Practice across Andean Worlds*

Asylum for Sale: Profit and Protest in the Migration Industry

Edited by Siobhán McGuirk &
Adrienne Pine with a Foreword by
Seth M. Holmes

ISBN: 978-1-62963-782-2
Price: $27.95   368 pages

This explosive new volume brings together a
lively cast of academics, activists, journalists, artists, and people directly
impacted by asylum regimes to explain how current practices of asylum
align with the neoliberal moment and to present their transformative
visions for alternative systems and processes.

Through essays, artworks, photographs, infographics, and illustrations,
Asylum for Sale: Profit and Protest in the Migration Industry regards the
global asylum regime as an industry characterized by profit-making
activity: brokers who facilitate border crossings for a fee; contractors
and firms that erect walls, fences, and watchtowers while lobbying
governments for bigger "security" budgets; corporations running
private detention centers and "managing" deportations; private lawyers
charging exorbitant fees; "expert" witnesses; and NGO staff establishing
careers while placing asylum seekers into new regimes of monitored
vulnerability.

Asylum for Sale challenges readers to move beyond questions of legal,
moral, and humanitarian obligations that dominate popular debates
regarding asylum seekers. Digging deeper, the authors focus on
processes and actors often overlooked in mainstream analyses and on
the trends increasingly rendering asylum available only to people with
financial and cultural capital. Probing every aspect of the asylum process
from crossings to aftermaths, the book provides an in-depth exploration
of complex, international networks, policies, and norms that impact
people seeking asylum around the world.

*"As the frontiers of disaster capitalism expand, the same systems that drive
migration are finding ever-more harrowing ways to criminalize and exploit
the displaced. This book is part of how we fight back: connecting the
extraordinary stories and insights of people studying, personally navigating,
and creatively resisting the global asylum industry. An unparalleled
resource."*
—Naomi Klein, author of *On Fire: The Burning Case for the Green New Deal*

The Art of Freedom: A Brief History of the Kurdish Liberation Struggle

Havin Guneser with an Introduction by Andrej Grubačić and Interview by Sasha Lilley

ISBN: 978-1-62963-781-5 (paperback)
       978-1-62963-907-9 (hardcover)
$16.95/$39.95   192 pages

The Revolution in Rojava captured the imagination of the Left sparking a worldwide interest in the Kurdish Freedom Movement. *The Art of Freedom* demonstrates that this explosive movement is firmly rooted in several decades of organized struggle.

In 2018, one of the most important spokespersons for the struggle of Kurdish Freedom, Havin Guneser, held three groundbreaking seminars on the historical background and guiding ideology of the movement. Much to the chagrin of career academics, the theoretical foundation of the Kurdish Freedom Movement is far too fluid and dynamic to be neatly stuffed into an ivory-tower filing cabinet. A vital introduction to the Kurdish struggle, *The Art of Freedom* is the first English-language book to deliver a distillation of the ideas and sensibilities that gave rise to the most important political event of the twenty-first century.

The book is broken into three sections: "Critique and Self-Critique: The rise of the Kurdish freedom movement from the rubbles of two world wars" provides an accessible explanation of the origins and theoretical foundation of the movement. "The Rebellion of the Oldest Colony: Jineology—the Science of Women" describes the undercurrents and nuance of the Kurdish women's movement and how they have managed to create the most vibrant and successful feminist movement in the Middle East. "Democratic Confederalism and Democratic Nation: Defense of Society Against Societycide" deals with the attacks on the fabric of society and new concepts beyond national liberation to counter it. Centering on notions of "a shared homeland" and "a nation made up of nations," these rousing ideas find deep international resonation.

Havin Guneser has provided an expansive definition of freedom and democracy and a road map to help usher in a new era of struggle against capitalism, imperialism, and the State.

Liberating Sápmi: Indigenous Resistance in Europe's Far North

Gabriel Kuhn

ISBN: 978-1-62963-712-9
$17.00   220 pages

The Sámi, who have inhabited Europe's far north for thousands of years, are often referred to as the continent's "forgotten people." With Sápmi, their traditional homeland, divided between four nation-states—Norway, Sweden, Finland, and Russia—the Sámi have experienced the profound oppression and discrimination that characterize the fate of indigenous people worldwide: their lands have been confiscated, their beliefs and values attacked, their communities and families torn apart. Yet the Sámi have shown incredible resilience, defending their identity and their territories and retaining an important social and ecological voice—even if many, progressives and leftists included, refuse to listen.

Liberating Sápmi is a stunning journey through Sápmi and includes in-depth interviews with Sámi artists, activists, and scholars boldly standing up for the rights of their people. In this beautifully illustrated work, Gabriel Kuhn, author of over a dozen books and our most fascinating interpreter of global social justice movements, aims to raise awareness of the ongoing fight of the Sámi for justice and self-determination. The first accessible English-language introduction to the history of the Sámi people and the first account that focuses on their political resistance, this provocative work gives irrefutable evidence of the important role the Sámi play in the resistance of indigenous people against an economic and political system whose power to destroy all life on earth has reached a scale unprecedented in the history of humanity.

The book contains interviews with Mari Boine, Harald Gaski, Ann-Kristin Håkansson, Aslak Holmberg, Maxida Märak, Stefan Mikaelsson, May-Britt Öhman, Synnøve Persen, Øyvind Ravna, Niillas Somby, Anders Sunna, and Suvi West.

Building Free Life: Dialogues with Öcalan

Edited by International Initiative

ISBN: 978-1-62963-704-4 (paperback)
       978-1-62963-764-8 (hardcover)
$20.00/$49.95   256 pages

From Socrates to Antonio Gramsci, imprisoned philosophers have marked the history of thought and changed how we view power and politics. From his solitary jail cell, Abdullah Öcalan has penned daringly innovative works that give profuse evidence of his position as one of the most significant thinkers of our day. His prison writings have mobilized tens of thousands of people and inspired a revolution in the making in Rojava, northern Syria, while also penetrating the insular walls of academia and triggering debate and reflection among countless scholars.

So how do you engage in a meaningful dialogue with Abdullah Öcalan when he has been held in total isolation since April 2015? You compile a book of essays written by a globally diverse cast of the most imaginative luminaries of our time, send it to Öcalan's jailers, and hope that they deliver it to him.

Featured in this extraordinary volume are over a dozen writers, activists, dreamers, and scholars whose ideas have been investigated in Öcalan's own writings. Now these same people have the unique opportunity to enter into a dialogue with his ideas. *Building Free Life* is a rich and wholly original exploration of the most critical issues facing humanity today. In the broad sweep of this one-of-a-kind dialogue, the contributors explore topics ranging from democratic confederalism to women's revolution, from the philosophy of history to the crisis of the capitalist system, from religion to Marxism and anarchism, all in an effort to better understand the liberatory social forms that are boldly confronting capitalism and the state.

There can be no boundaries or restrictions for the development of thought. Thus, in the midst of different realities—from closed prisons to open-air prisons—the human mind will find a way to seek the truth. *Building Free Life* stands as a monument of radical thought, a testament of resilience, and a searchlight illuminating the impulse for freedom.

Re-enchanting the World: Feminism and the Politics of the Commons

Silvia Federici
with a Foreword by Peter Linebaugh

ISBN: 978-1-62963-569-9
$19.95   256 pages

Silvia Federici is one of the most important contemporary theorists of capitalism and feminist movements. In this collection of her work spanning over twenty years, she provides a detailed history and critique of the politics of the commons from a feminist perspective. In her clear and combative voice, Federici provides readers with an analysis of some of the key issues and debates in contemporary thinking on this subject.

Drawing on rich historical research, she maps the connections between the previous forms of enclosure that occurred with the birth of capitalism and the destruction of the commons and the "new enclosures" at the heart of the present phase of global capitalist accumulation. Considering the commons from a feminist perspective, this collection centers on women and reproductive work as crucial to both our economic survival and the construction of a world free from the hierarchies and divisions capital has planted in the body of the world proletariat. Federici is clear that the commons should not be understood as happy islands in a sea of exploitative relations but rather autonomous spaces from which to challenge the existing capitalist organization of life and labor.

"Silvia Federici's theoretical capacity to articulate the plurality that fuels the contemporary movement of women in struggle provides a true toolbox for building bridges between different features and different people."
—Massimo De Angelis, professor of political economy, University of East London

"Silvia Federici's work embodies an energy that urges us to rejuvenate struggles against all types of exploitation and, precisely for that reason, her work produces a common: a common sense of the dissidence that creates a community in struggle."
—Maria Mies, coauthor of *Ecofeminism*

We Are the Crisis of Capital:
A John Holloway Reader

John Holloway

ISBN: 978-1-62963-225-4
$22.95   320 pages

We Are the Crisis of Capital collects articles and excerpts written by radical academic, theorist, and activist John Holloway over a period of forty years.

WE
A
ARE
John Holloway
THE
CRISIS
Reader
OF
JOHN HOLLOWAY
CAPITAL

Different times, different places, and the same anguish persists throughout our societies. This collection asks, "Is there a way out?" How do we break capital, a form of social organisation that dehumanises us and threatens to annihilate us completely? How do we create a world based on the mutual recognition of human dignity?

Holloway's work answers loudly, "By screaming NO!" By thinking from our own anger and from our own creativity. By trying to recover the "We" who are buried under the categories of capitalist thought. By opening the categories and discovering the antagonism they conceal, by discovering that behind the concepts of money, state, capital, crisis, and so on, there moves our resistance and rebellion.

An approach sometimes referred to as Open Marxism, it is an attempt to rethink Marxism as daily struggle. The articles move forward, influenced by the German state derivation debates of the seventies, by the CSE debates in Britain, and the group around the Edinburgh journal *Common Sense*, and then moving on to Mexico and the wonderful stimulus of the Zapatista uprising, and now the continuing whirl of discussion with colleagues and students in the Posgrado de Sociología of the Benemérita Universidad Autónoma de Puebla.

"Holloway's work is infectiously optimistic."
—Steven Poole, the *Guardian* (UK)

"Holloway's thesis is indeed important and worthy of notice."
—Richard J.F. Day, *Canadian Journal of Cultural Studies*

KAIROS

In ancient Greek philosophy, *kairos* signifies the right time or the "moment of transition." We believe that we live in such a transitional period. The most important task of social science in time of transformation is to transform itself into a force of liberation. Kairos, an editorial imprint of the Anthropology and Social Change department housed in the California Institute of Integral Studies, publishes groundbreaking works in critical social sciences, including anthropology, sociology, geography, theory of education, political ecology, political theory, and history.

Series editor: Andrej Grubačić

Recent and featured Kairos books:

Autonomy Is in Our Hearts: Zapatista Autonomous Government through the Lens of the Tsotsil Language by Dylan Eldredge Fitzwater

Building Free Life: Dialogues with Öcalan edited by International Initiative

The Art of Freedom: A Brief History of the Kurdish Liberation Struggle by Havin Guneser

The Sociology of Freedom: Manifesto of the Democratic Civilization, Volume III by Abdullah Öcalan

The Battle for the Mountain of the Kurds: Self-Determination and Ethnic Cleansing in the Afrin Region of Rojava by Thomas Schmidinger

Taming the Rascal Multitude: Essays, Interviews, and Lectures 1997–2014 by Noam Chomsky

A New World in Our Hearts: Noam Chomsky in Conversation with Michael Albert

Between Thought and Expression Lies a Lifetime: Why Ideas Matter by Noam Chomsky and James Kelman

Mutual Aid: An Illuminated Factor of Evolution by Peter Kropotkin, illustrated by N.O. Bonzo

For more information visit www.pmpress.org/blog/kairos/

"Since they first captured my attention in 1994, the EZLN's struggle and the writings of Subcomandante Marcos/Galeano have been a constant source of hope and inspiration. During our current time of monsters, the stories that form this wonderful 'accidental archive of Zapatista struggle' invite us to once again embrace radical hope, to work for futures not yet born, and to affirm yet again that other, more just, worlds are indeed possible. Revolutions have come and gone, to paraphrase Emiliano Zapata, and the EZLN keep on with theirs."
—Alexander Aviña, author of *Specters of Revolution: Peasant Guerrillas in the Cold War Mexican Countryside* (2014)

"*Zapatista Stories for Dreaming An-Other World* is more than the English translation of *Los Otros Cuentos*, written by Subcomandante Insurgente Marcos. It is a poetic and political dialogue between Zapatista thought and the historical contextualization of a group of activist translators inspired by the struggles of the Indigenous peoples from Chiapas. The members of the Colectivo Relámpago (Lightning Collective) make a hermeneutic reading of the Zapatista fables, from a profound knowledge of the stories of resistance in the Maya region."
—R. Aída Hernández Castillo, author of *Multiple (In) Justices: Indigenous Woman, Law and Political Struggle in Latin America* (2016) and *Descolonizando el Feminismo: Teorías y Prácticas desde los Márgenes* (2008)

"On January 1, 1994, the Zapatista Army of National Liberation not only had the nerve to stare down the proclaimed End of History and launch a war against the Mexican government, a war against neoliberalism, and a war against racial and patriarchal capitalism in all its forms—while, in the process, recuperating tens of thousands of acres of land that was stolen from the Indigenous peoples of Chiapas—but they did all this with a sense of humor, with poetry, and with, in a word, literature. *Zapatista Stories for Dreaming An-Other World*, expertly translated by the Colectivo Relámpago, offers an excellent introduction to, and commentary on, the vast anti-archive of the Zapatistas' *other* literature."
—John Gibler, author of *I Couldn't Even Imagine They Would Kill Us: An Oral History of the Attacks against the Students of Ayotzinapa* (2017) and *To Die in Mexico: Dispatches from Inside the Drug War* (2011)

"Thinking through the heart. This collection reminds, (re)grounds, and expands our collective sense of possibility— as the Zapatistas so creatively have continued to do for over twenty-seven years. From the alter-globalization movements to the horizontal assemblies in Argentina of the early 2000s through Occupy and the Movements of the Squares in the 2010s to our pandemic solidarities and mutual aid networks in the 2020s, prefigurative, autonomous, and affective movements continue to move with the Zapatistas in our hearts and minds. The influence and inspiration are beyond words, yet this collection gives words, placing crucial stories of the Zapatista communities in historical context, giving us more lenses through which to see the world and our movements within it."
—Marina Sitrin, author of *Pandemic Solidarity: Mutual Aid during the COVID 19 Crisis* (2020) and *They Can't Represent Us! Reinventing Democracy from Greece to Occupy* (2014)

"This is a beautiful, inspired project. In a joyful Zapatista gesture that all readers will welcome, this volume invites us to play, to walk on different, and even contrary, paths through smooth and crystalline translations that bring these *Other Stories* to life. The translators' commentaries preserve a delicate balance of expertise and autonomy, as they illuminate the historical, political, and cultural forces that provoked the stories' creation. Among these forces are Zapatista women, whom the translators rightly dignify in their meticulous and provocative introduction. This volume is a gift to so many of us as we (attempt to) bring the Zapatista imagination to our students and organizing communities."
—Michelle Joffroy, associate professor of Spanish and Latin American and Latino Studies, Smith College, and codirector of Domestic Workers Make History, www.dwherstories.com

"From the beating heart of Mesoamerica, the old gods speak to us through the tales of Old Antonio, while a glasses-wearing, pipe-smoking beetle brings it all back to Western discourse, as together they entice us to share the Zapatistas' revolutionary struggles from below and to the left. The Colectivo Relámpago (Lightning Collective), based in Amherst, Massachusetts, translates and comments with bolts of illumination zigzagging across cultures and nations, bringing bursts of laughter and sudden charges of hot-wired political energy. It seems like child's play, yet it's almost divine!"
—Peter Linebaugh, author of *Red Round Globe Hot Burning* (2019)